THERE SHE GLOWS

VOLUME III

LUCY CRANE
STACEY KNIGHT-JONES

CONTENTS

INTRODUCTION

She was held by the earth, moved by the moon, sparked by the sun,
swayed by the sea.
She already had the answers within her, she always had done.
She was already enough, she always had been.
But she had just learned to forget.
And as she chose to surrender she learned to trust herself and her
intuition once more.
She was able to shift her thoughts from fear to love,
And in doing so experience her own miracles.
And just like the sun, the stars, and the moon she glowed a little bit
differently but in her own unique way.
She no longer allowed the opinions of others who lacked courage in their
own dreams to discourage her own.
She was able to step into her highest purpose and potential radiating
self-love and acceptance.
She was in a place where she could gain clarity on her intentions with
the confidence to follow through.

And in remembering she realised the journey was never about becoming anything but rather unbecoming everything that was never really her, to be who she was always meant to be.

And in saying YES to herself, she left her old stories behind her and stepped into a new once upon a time.

A place where her soul was lit and her dreams were realised.

A place where she was able to share her gifts,

And in her own unique way shake the world.

A place that allowed her to come home to who she truly was and allowed her to breathe again.

She was home.

So now it's time to let go of the past, trust in the future and embrace change.

Be brave enough to come out of your cocoon, unfurl your wings and dare to get off the ground wearing your brightest colours.

Let your beauty show.

You were born to do wonderful things, so believe in yourself and dare to dream again.

The power is within you to be the change in the world you were always meant to be.

Welcome to Glow Society,
Our Mission & Message

"Lighting Up the World One Woman at a Time"

Welcome to the third Volume of the 'There She Glows' book collaborations. Following the beautiful success and inspiration of the women who fearlessly led Volume 1 and 2 with so much love, inspiration, and truth. Glow Society as a company truly believes that every woman should have the opportunity to share their message and unique gifts to the world in their own way, knowing that in doing so, it will allow you to feel less alone in your world. We know you have been guided here for a reason. There will be certain lessons, blessings, words of wisdom, and encouragement that you have been waiting to hear that can shine a light for you, wherever you are on your journey.

There will be some of you who have already embraced the love and light of Volume One and Two of our There She Glows Book Collaborations, whilst for others, this may be the very first time you have been guided to find us. Partnered with 12 incredible women from around the world, we want to take this opportunity to thank them all for their beautiful and courageous contributions. For choosing love over fear and having the courage to share their truth, their message, lessons, and blessings to inspire and empower the rest of the world. We have complete love and gratitude for them all and between them, we know they will support you, our reader, in realising the highest and most inspired vision for your life and your future. It is a huge privilege to be able to provide a platform for these incredible women to truly share their light with you all. Each and every chapter is uniquely beautiful as our co-authors share their own journeys, embracing the evolution of the women they have truly become. This evolution is one that continues in each and every one of our lives, and as a company, we can absolutely reflect this in our own journey. Together we are creating a movement and through our Global Membership, Coaching, Retreats, Workshops, and Life Coaching Certification we support women to finally

BREAK FREE, and Create the Abundant Lifestyle and Business they truly dream of.

Our vision is to ensure that every woman with dreams gives herself permission to live her purpose so as a collective we can raise the vibration and bring more happiness, love and light into the world.

We want to gift every woman with the confidence to know her self- worth, the strength to chase her dreams, and the ability to know how deeply loved, worthy, and capable she is of creating a life she loves. One that is led by alignment, intuition and soul and allows her to be a beacon of light for others. As we individually GLOW one person at a time, we can truly light up the world.

 "When we know how to access our inner light, we glow from the inside out and everything outside of us can GLOW with us."

— GLOW SOCIETY

An invitation from us to you with love....

THE STORY OF THE STARFISH

"One day, an old man was walking along a beach that was littered with thousands of starfish that had been washed ashore by the high tide. As he walked he came upon a young boy who was eagerly throwing the starfish back into the ocean, one by one.
Puzzled, the man looked at the boy and asked what he was doing.

Without looking up from his task, the boy simply replied, "I'm saving these starfish, Sir".
The old man chuckled aloud, "Son, there are thousands of starfish and only one of you. What difference can you make?"
The boy picked up a starfish, gently tossed it into the water, and turning to the man, said, "I made a difference to that one!"
- Loren Eiseley

This beautiful story highlights the ripples we can all create together to impact the lives of many.

As women with dreams, wearing our many hats, we appreciate how you may be feeling and how you truly desire to feel. FREE……Financially, physically, emotionally, and spiritually and just know wherever you are on your journey we are here to be your daily hug, daily guide, and daily go-to so that creating your dreams no longer feels out of reach, overwhelming, or too big.

The magic of wanting to live and be like you never thought you could is never really about the destination, it's about the journey and the woman you become in the process and together we can truly embrace this (for further details about everything we provide to support women here at Glow, head to the Bio section).

WE VALUE:

FAMILY.
"Where life begins and love never ends."

AUTHENTICITY.

"Unbecoming everything that was never really you to be who you were always meant to be."

FREEDOM.

"The opportunity to be, and live like you never thought you could."

CONTRIBUTION.

"People will forget what you did, people will forget what you said but they will never forget how you made them feel."

PURPOSE TO IMPACT THE WORLD.

"In a gentle way, you can shake the world."

LOVING RELATIONSHIPS.

"To be part of a community that enables you to feel less alone."

UNCOMPROMISED DREAMS.

"Let your dreams be bigger than your fears, and actions be louder than your words."

MAKING MEMORIES.

"Live for the moments we can't put into words. We don't remember the days; we remember the memories."

A LIFE FULL OF CHOICES.

"Is a life well-lived."

FAITH.

"The confidence in what we hope for, and assurance about what we don't see."

And more importantly, we value YOU.

Please know how valued, appreciated, and loved you are as one of our readers from around the world and remember you always have the power to create your own MIRACLES.

"To live is the rarest thing in the world, most people just exist,"

— OSCAR WILDE

…And you my darling deserve to truly live.
So let today be the first day of the rest of your life!

WELCOME TO THE DOORS OF GLOW SOCIETY

We have ONE Mission –

 *'To Light Up The World, One Woman at a Time By Empowering Them To Transform Their Own Lives.'*

Through our Global Membership, Coaching, Retreats, Workshops, and Life Coaching Certification we support women to finally **BREAK FREE** and Create the Abundant Lifestyle and Business they truly dream of.

Our vision is to ensure that every woman with dreams gives herself permission to live her purpose so as a collective we can raise the vibration and bring more happiness, love and light into the world. We want to gift every woman with the confidence to know her self-worth, the strength to chase her dreams, and the ability to know how deeply loved, worthy and capable she is of creating a life she loves.

JOIN THE GLOW SOCIETY MEMBERSHIP:

Our Membership provides your Daily 'go-to', & Life Coach in your pocket (without the Coaching investment) as you navigate through the waves of life. We provide the Life and Spiritual Coaching tools, Community, Personal Development, Well-being, Emotional Resilience (in every area of your life), Hypnotherapy, Courses & Transformations from the inside out to support women to re-balance, re-align, and re-fill their cups so that they are so full, they're overflowing daily. We focus on supporting women to transition into their dreams, purpose and potential. We will empower every single woman to truly GLOW.

It's time to:

- Breathe life back into you and your dreams - *because you are worthy… worthy of it all.*
- Finally BREAK FREE - *free from the beliefs, the habits, the negative emotions that until now have been keeping you stuck.*
- Learn Our 5 Step Process to Reigniting your GLOW and Creating all that your heart desires- the money, the love, *the Business, the Health, the Freedom, the Happiness and Success.*
- Master your Emotions - *jump off the emotional rollercoaster so that you can experience what life is meant to feel like.*
- Gain the confidence and clarity in your life and business - *to truly find your place in the world and what that looks like for you.*

- Feed Your Inner Glow daily - *in every area of your life so that you can fill your cup so full that it's overflowing.*
- Find and live your purpose in alignment with your values and joy - *so that you can live with more intention and meaning.*
- Connect to your truth and higher self with the spiritual tools - *to radiate in self-love, self-worth and acceptance.*

Finally, believe in you and your dreams once again. Because you my darling are worthy of it all.

You can join The Glow Society Membership for just £1.11 today and watch how your world and all you are currently experiencing it to be changes with you: www.glow-society.com

GLOW RETREATS AND WORKSHOPS:

Our Retreats and Workshops create a 'belly to belly' community and space to escape, rest, release, connect, and heal whilst experiencing real transformations at an unconscious level, spiritual healings, workshops, & fun adventures that make memories and friendships that last a lifetime. For more information on our upcoming retreats visit: www.glow-society.com

**COACHING COLLECTIVE -
BECOME A CERTIFIED LIFE COACH:**

There has never been a more expansive moment in history to communicate your gifts. To bring freedom and joy to others, whilst creating your own financial abundance, joy, and freedom standing in your purpose.

We are an Internationally Recognised Training Facilitator, to both Aspiring, and Current Coaches, and provide a guiding light for Personal Transformation, Soulful Awakening, Aligned Strategy, and the freedom for Women to truly GLOW into their Purpose, Potential and Dreams.

Our Life Coaching Certification programme supports our coaching students to fearlessly launch their calling, evoke their spiritual gifts, and embody personal Transformation with the skills, unshakable foundations, energetic blueprint, love, and support to launch, and grow purpose-driven, and abundant Coaching business, whilst creating a lifestyle of Freedom, Happiness and Fulfilment.

We Provide:
Energetically Aligned Coaching Methodologies, Mindset, & Business Strategy.
We Trust:
The power of Spirit & Soul Meeting Strategy & Purpose.
We Embody:
The Yin & the Yang to Life, Business, & Coaching Mastery.
We Leverage:
The Magic of Intuition, Alignment & Energy Alchemy.

Find out More About Joining Our Coaching Collective:
More Information on our Unique opportunity for Coaching students to become Certified Coaches can be found on our website at: www.glow-society.com

MEET YOUR FOUNDERS

Lucy Crane

Accredited Master Coach & Trainer (IAPC&M Accredited - Master Coach Training Course Level-7), 4x Best Selling Author, Retreat Leader, NLP Practitioner, Theta Healer, Hypnotherapist & Founder of the 'There She Glows' Collaboration Books.

Stacey Knight-Jones

Mindfulness Expert, Retreat Leader, Transformational Life & Purpose Coach, Personal Development Junkie, Hypnotherapist, NLP Practitioner, 2x Best Selling Author & Co-founder of the 'There She Glows' Collaboration Books.

You will find us collectively sharing all of our free gifts and value over on *Youtube so do come over and hit the subscribe button to access many more resources to support you to truly change your life!*

FIND OUR CHANNEL ON YOUTUBE: 'GLOW SOCIETY™

https://www.youtube.com/channel/Glow Society™

COMPLIMENT YOUR JOURNEY WITH OUR FEED YOUR INNER GLOW JOURNAL:

https://www.amazon.co.uk/dp/B09TN1GGZ5

Connect With Us Further

Website: www.glow-society.com

Youtube:

https://www.youtube.com/channel/GlowSociety™

Membership: www.glow-society.com

Instagram: we_are_glow_society

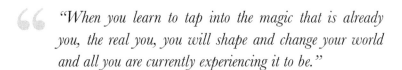

"When you learn to tap into the magic that is already you, the real you, you will shape and change your world and all you are currently experiencing it to be."

— GLOW SOCIETY

We wish you so much success, love, and light in all that you do,
Luc, Stace & the Glow Team

THE JOURNEY TO AN ALIGNED LIFE

CARLI THORPE

*H*ave you ever reached a point in your life where you came to a grinding halt? A moment where you simply couldn't carry on for a moment longer? This was me, at the age of 37, a seemingly healthy and happy individual. I was walking across campus to a meeting that I never arrived at. Half way there, I completely crumbled - physically, mentally, emotionally and spiritually. My body was making sure, in no uncertain terms that I stopped and listened.

In hindsight, my body had been whispering to me for months. I ignored the signals, disregarding my symptoms as random, unrelated to my life. I pushed through until one day I stopped being able to function. Feeling broken beyond words and deeply frightened, I did the only thing I could: I surrendered.

The following weeks were a blur. A deep heaviness, fog and exhaustion had set into my entire being. I was emotionally distraught and incredibly lost. Given a clean bill of physical health, I was signed off sick, but was offered no solutions. Since the moment of surrender, there had been the quietest inner voice saying "follow me". With no other viable options from the outside world, I began to follow that inner voice. Little did I know it was guiding me on a profound journey of healing and self-discovery.

As my strength returned, a gradual clarity came with it. That I had some tough choices to make about my life and the way I was living it. In short, I could stay living in a way that was, fundamentally, wrong for *me*, or change it. I chose to change it.

Back then I couldn't have told you how my life would change. I just knew change was paramount. Through trusting that inner voice, today my life is an ever deepening tapestry of discovery, connection and meaning. My inner and outer worlds have transformed beyond recognition. The depth to which I experience life is profound. I am guided by an inner compass, a felt sense in my body that previously didn't exist. I feel free, with a renewed sense of Self and vitality. I have the capacity to feel it *ALL*.

In taking steps to heal from the past and change what was out of alignment in my life, I have, in truth, come home to myself. In awakening my mind, body and spirit connection, I have built a relationship with my Self that brings with it an absolute knowing of my place in the world, a belonging that previously had been alien to me. I now navigate life with purpose and intentionality in a way that is true to me.

When I look back at who I was, I see someone leading the kind of life you would imagine. I'd get up, go to work. Do my job. Come home. Make dinner. Watch TV. Go to bed. There would be enjoyable social events. I had a house. A car. A husband. A career. Two holidays a year. I had plans to have children and therefore to stay in my safe job and successful career for the maternity pay and the pension. I would remain in this perfect life and all would be well. I had all the things that are *supposed* to make you happy.

Yet, there was a niggle. Something was off. This niggle was barely audible and I ignored it, became numb to it… until June 2017, the point of major burnout when I was forced to finally listen.

The first signs of burnout were towards the end of 2016. I was struggling with work. The projects I managed were big, complicated and high profile. Yes, I was good at it *and* at the same time it was taking its toll on me. My heart wasn't in it. Not anymore.

To add complication, I was also trying to fall pregnant. I was trying to hold it all together and show the world I had it all figured out, that everything was ok. Even though the cracks were starting to show, I was in denial to myself and all those around me. Underneath this slowly crumbling facade was deep rooted fear that if I admitted the truth of how I was *really* feeling, I would be admitting failure at life; I would be rejected and my life would fall apart.

The second pivotal moment came when I learned it was highly unlikely that I would fall pregnant. I was devastated. I'd been so wrapped up in the story of having the perfect life, which included becoming a mum and it was torn away from me. Through the grief, came eventual clarity and an absolute truth: It was time to create a life that I loved, with or without becoming a mum. I had absolutely no idea what that meant or where to start.

In this journey of 'fixing' my outer world, the real transformation was taking place in my inner world. It was messy and painful. It gradually became clear that peace would come with letting go of the past, of all that wasn't *me* and creating a life aligned with my heart.

My body had been calling me to this all along. The whispers had started quietly, and through my fear, numbness and denial, it took for them to become incredibly loud for me to finally listen.

You see, the body's innate wisdom far exceeds the capacity that the mind can comprehend. Our entire experience is stored in our body. A history of everything. Every thought, feeling, belief and emotion. And our body is always communicating with us. The question is, are we listening? I had no idea back then that *all* of my symptoms were, in fact, meaningful and decipherable messages – the physiology of my life journey mapped out waiting to be interpreted.

Sometime later, I stumbled upon metaphysical anatomy, the concept that illness and dis-ease has its roots in emotional conflict. When I applied the theory to my own health, and later supporting others to do the same, it all made perfect sense. My understanding of illness and dis-ease was completely transformed. Combining this knowledge with the immense healing capacity of energy work and physical movement practices, I knew I had stumbled upon a unique combination with the power to change lives – including my own.

From a very young age I believed I had to be like everyone else to be accepted. Conforming, compliance and obedience were paramount to my survival. It's no wonder I chose conventional routes in life; anything that created a *safe and acceptable existence*. My subconscious was expertly driving patterns of behaviour and choices based on this need and all of the limiting beliefs I had to go with it.

I believed the story ingrained in many of us - that life is about growing up, getting a job, getting married, having the house and the car, having children and living happily ever after. Add to this my determination to do it better than witnessed through my own childhood experience and you have a recipe for perfectionism, people pleasing, high levels of stress and a striving for over-achievement.

But, there was a major flaw in this plan of mine. I wasn't *perfect*, and because I wasn't *perfect* I was doing it wrong. I wasn't good enough. I wasn't doing enough. I wasn't smart or pretty enough. All the *not enough-ness* you can imagine. I felt it. With the understanding I have now - how our external life experience is a reflection of, and a vibrational match to our inner world - I can also see how I was perpetuating more of the same. I was collecting evidence that these things were true. Unable to live up to this fabricated perception of perfection, I had crippling low self-confidence and self-worth, zero self-belief and I hated myself.

At the same time, I also carried around this deep feeling of being different. Highly sensitive, empathic and deeply caring, I couldn't make sense of the world around me. It felt unsafe and it didn't match what I felt inside. Confused and angry, everything about me felt wrong. Believing I had to conform for acceptance was a direct conflict to how different I knew I was. This meant I had a big secret to keep - along with a bucket-load of guilt. If anyone found out, surely I would be rejected? I was already rejecting myself in many ways, so it made sense to me that others would too. On the outside I was trying to live up to expectations and on the inside I felt deeply sad, lost and afraid.

On my mission to fit in and be perfect, I was one of those children that got on well with everyone and everything - I made sure I did! Although I would have denied it vehemently at the time, I was good at everything I did. I was a musician in the school orchestra; I danced and performed in shows; I took part in school plays and sports days. I enjoyed it all, and yet my passion – especially for music and dance - was curbed by the undercurrent of everything I felt inside.

This mission carried through to my working life and relationships. I always did everything to the best of my ability and in the way I believed would *most please other people*.

In work and relationships, I was a 'yes' person, making sure I not only met but exceeded expectations. I had become an expert at morphing myself into who I believed others expected me to be. I was being everyone other than my Self and I was incapable of saying no. That meant the work piled up, the responsibility increased and the roles I was playing became more complex - and so did the stress.

Yes, there were achievements that I am proud of. I won awards at work and was entered into leadership programmes. Encouraged to climb the ladder. I was a rising star. An employee with potential. All this sounds great – except I never stopped to think whether it was what I wanted. It didn't occur to me I had a choice! Disconnected from myself, I just went with what came my way and kept hidden the fear and beliefs that I didn't deserve it, wasn't worthy of it and one day people would figure out the truth!

No surprise then, that in my teens I was diagnosed with depression and anxiety, and eventually, in my early twenties, medicated for it. What I was feeling was too big, too painful and too difficult. The stress I was putting myself under meant I simply couldn't cope with daily life.

Where, might you ask, did all of these beliefs and feelings come from?

Why did I have crippling low self-confidence, zero self-worth, non-existent self-belief and an abundance of self-hatred? Why did I constantly strive for this illusion of perfection, and why did I repeatedly allow unacceptable behaviour in relationships? Why did I feel that everything about me was wrong? Why was I incapable and terrified of saying no? Why was I in this place of constant self-rejection and self-criticism? Why couldn't I believe in myself the way that other people did? Why couldn't I see what others could see in me?

I could spend an inordinately large amount of time writing about my childhood experiences. How we, tragically, lost one of my brothers to leukemia at a very young age with a devastating impact on my family. I could share about instability in my home life through my early and formative years, including my parents' divorce and the events that followed. I could also talk about being born into a family with a history of mental health challenges and how we each developed numbing and coping mechanisms.

All of these experiences are, without doubt, fundamental to the person I became, the beliefs I formed about myself and the world around me. However, I cannot emphasise enough how it was my *perception* of these experiences and how I *responded to them* that was the key. It is the perception that creates emotional conflict in our physiology. How we respond to it denotes whether we fully heal from the experience. You might think I am being hard on myself, expecting my childhood self to have perceived these experiences as anything other than traumatic. Let me assure you, there are no judgements here – simply reflections of my experiences then, based on what I now know.

Two people can be in the same room, participating in the same experience, yet perceive it and respond completely differently. How do I know this? Partly through my studies, and most significantly through experience - because I am a twin! My twin and I shared many of the same experiences, especially in our early years. Yet we each perceived and responded to them differently. I believe there are many factors to this. Partly, what we are born into this world with – our life lessons, Soul wounds and ancestral lineage; partly how we are treated by others (as the only female of four, I was, whether consciously or not, treated differently to my brothers) and among other factors, how empathic or highly sensitive we are. I am a highly sensitive person. I have discovered with energy techniques, that I am a sponge for absorbing what is going on in the environment around me. Pre-medication, I didn't just feel *my* emotions – I also felt everyone else's! This was a huge realisation. Can you imagine how this might feel for a child? I had no way (until recently) to discern what was mine and not mine and I had been collecting this stuff for years!

My perception created my reality – as is true for us all. In the words of Henry David Thoreau, "it's not what you look at that matters, it is what you see". What I saw was everything wrong with me. The result was self-rejection wrapped in layers of guilt, shame, anger, hurt, protectionism and perfectionism. I was hiding my true self from the world because the real me was, as I believed it, entirely unacceptable.

Temporary respite came as I entered my mid-teens and discovered alcohol, drugs and all-night raves - a period of blissful escapism. Those years are very fond memories, not least because it was my twin brother DJ'ing creating a euphoric atmosphere. In that space, everything was wonderful. I didn't have a care in the world. My weekends, for a time at least, became a blur of hedonistic joy. But that is not a sustainable lifestyle!

All of these beliefs, along with the confidence, self-worth and self-belief crisis would continue to play out in my life – not least in relationships with men. In my desperation to be accepted and loved, I would morph into whomever I was in a relationship with. My non-existent boundaries meant I would accept appalling treatment, including, in earlier relationships, mental abuse and threats of physical violence. Each time, I would eventually leave. Not being able to say no meant leaving was the only way I could stand up for myself. I would walk away feeling exhausted, hurt and disappointed. Little did I know these experiences were simply a reflection of how I felt about myself.

Now, I can see how not recognising my worth, not accepting and loving myself, meant I couldn't love and accept another - not in a healthy way. I also couldn't receive the unconditional love of another all the while I was rejecting and hiding myself. Until recently, this concept had been a mystery to me. This, I believe, is one of the contributing factors to my marriage breakdown in 2019.

All of this manifested in prolonged episodes of anxiety and depression. During my darkest moments I wished desperately that I hadn't been born. Suicide was never an option because death was one of my greatest fears and a source of intense anxiety. I felt trapped, living in this cruel and painful world with no way out. I was medicated for much of my twenties and thirties, not knowing how else to function. It numbed the pain and dulled the intensity of *everything*. I attempted to wean myself off occasionally, only to experience the same debilitating symptoms again.

Back then, I believed anti-depressants were *curing* the depression. At the time of prescription I was told it is hereditary, irreversible with no causal link to my life experience, that my brain simply didn't produce enough serotonin. Within a few weeks of taking them, I could function again and resumed the illusion of perfection. The unbearable lows were gone but so too had my capacity to experience deep joy.

The medication was merely numbing me from the inside out. Masking the symptoms that my body was expertly creating as messengers, calling me to heal. A journey that wouldn't begin until 2016 when I made the choice to once-and-for-all taper from anti-depressants.

This decision to taper was motivated by the desire to become a mum. By this point, my life was seemingly sorted. There was no reason to be on the tablets anymore and it was time to get pregnant. After a well-planned and gradual taper, I was heartbroken to begin experiencing the same tell-tale signs of anxiety and depression.

It made no sense that these symptoms would re-occur. After all, my life was *perfect*. So, I began to research. I discovered relapse and withdrawal can manifest as the same symptoms. The research also revealed many possible contributing factors to my symptoms, ranging from the food I was eating, the chemicals I was ingesting and exposed to in my environment, and, not least the repressed emotions, unhealed wounds, and limiting beliefs I was carrying. I began to recognise depression and anxiety as symptoms, rather than as an irreversible disease and I was determined to *fix* it and *fix* me.

I was still oblivious to the enormity of what was to come and hadn't yet learned I probably couldn't conceive. In an attempt to make my symptoms go away as quickly as possible, I began a meditation practice. I embarked on dietary changes and detoxification programmes. I read every self-help book I could get my hands on. I began trying different types of therapy – hypnotherapy, timeline therapy, Cognitive Behavioural Therapy, Emotional Freedom Technique – tools that all played a very valuable part in my journey, but I was still approaching it all from the perspective of *making it go away*, rather than true resolution and healing.

During these months of trying to make my symptoms go away, I was, in truth, in avoidance. Avoiding what I was feeling and avoiding reality. I was slowly descending into a full-scale burnout. Those days are a blur to me. But I remember episodes of feeling emotionally bereft, hiding in the toilets at work, sobbing on the phone to my closest friend. Hyper-sensitive to noise, with no amount of sleep being enough, I was in a constant state of overwhelm. Simple instructions were becoming increasingly incomprehensible and the pressure felt immense.

Eventually I reached that pivotal moment in 2017. The moment when I could no longer function. I had reached the bottom of the pit and what I now recognise as the culmination point of everything. I was exhausted from a lifetime of perfectionism and living a false Self - presenting the versions of me that I perceived to be acceptable and palatable. And I simply couldn't do it anymore.

This total burnout was, unbeknown to me, the beginning of my *breakthrough*. The start of my journey to an aligned life.

Slowly and incrementally, I applied what I was learning. I started having regular acupuncture, practiced radical self-care and dropped into deep rest. I spent lots of time in nature and cried more tears than you can fathom – it was part of the letting go. I gradually came back to life. I had unwavering support from close friends and family, without whom I couldn't have taken these steps. And I somehow found the strength to overcome the resistance of those who didn't support my chosen path. I was starting to experience what it was to live in accordance with my own needs and values. I allowed the falling away of what and who were not in alignment with the real me to create space for what and who was.

In Spring 2018, I was back at work part-time and re-training as a Pilates Instructor – a movement modality that played a key role in overcoming debilitating back pain. Knowing that I wanted to help others with their health and wellbeing I began the training course – this was as good a place to start as any! I had no idea what a key part it would play in my alignment journey and what I now bring to others. At least not until I discovered the Energy Alignment Method (EAM®) – an incredible transformational technique and the next piece of the puzzle.

Using EAM alongside the understanding of metaphysical anatomy and physical movement practices, facilitated healing on a deep level. This technique and the supportive community were (and still are) paramount in the transformation of everything I have shared here. With this transformation came the gradual clarity of what was needed in order to create what I call an aligned life – living in harmony with the truth of who I am.

So pivotal in my journey and a non-negotiable in my daily self-care, I decided to train as an EAM Mentor, bringing another tool into the Alignment Toolkit I now share with others as an Intuitive Alignment Practitioner.

I was recently sitting at traffic lights in my camper van, driving home from a Pilates class, a 40+ woman, singing one of my favourite songs at the top of my voice, wearing a bright blue hat with fluffy bobbles, not caring in the slightest what others in adjacent cars were thinking, and I realised: I am freely living life my way. I felt so full of vitality and joy. I felt like *me*.

The tools, techniques and information I have learned and applied over the last five years (and continue to apply now) have facilitated this journey of returning home to myself and replenishing my health. Re-aligning physically, mentally, emotionally and spiritually, I live in harmony with *my* natural rhythms and cycles (rather than those imposed by society). In doing so, I am creating a life that doesn't look like the 'norm'. But it feels absolutely right for *me*.

The ability to discern what is and is not for me is growing. So too is my capacity to say no with ease! This discernment comes from a deep inner knowing. A felt sense and a presence within. It is my inner compass, my intuition guiding me through life. How I ever managed without it I do not know.

Unshackling myself from conditioning; transforming the limiting beliefs and patterns; healing the wounds of the past has given me the freedom, confidence and self-belief to step into my power and step out into the world doing what I know I am here to do! I feel an inner strength and knowing that our deepest wounds, when we commit to healing, become our greatest gifts.

Radical self-care and alignment are my top priority. Non-negotiable. I have my 'Alignment Toolkit' that I choose from each day. I am worth nothing less than this. When I am taking the greatest care of myself I am honouring the gifts I have been given; I can experience life with vitality and joy and I can be of the greatest service to others.

I now have the capacity to hold all of me and my experience. Connected to my emotions and no longer suppressing and bypassing them, I feel *everything*. Even the messy parts. My emotions help me navigate through life, showing me what I would like to create more of and what is there to be healed. In experiencing, processing and communicating emotions in a healthy way, I not only enrich my experience of life, but also prevent stress and unwanted physiological symptoms.

I see the world in an entirely different way now. Everything is a beautiful inter-connected web. What previously seemed random and chaotic, now has purpose and meaning. I am a part of that with a unique role to play. You are too!

No longer clinging, I allow and trust that which needs to fall away to do so, in order to create space for more of what is in alignment with the life I am creating.

The journey home to Self, and living *your* truth is one of great courage, deep inner listening, patience and discernment. It requires facing parts of yourself you may not like – and coming to accept them. Coming to unconditionally love *all* of you. It requires you to recognise the part you have played in your life experience so far, to take personal responsibility for it and heal from it. But it is also a journey of immense growth, expansion and freedom. One that means you live *on purpose*, with presence and deep appreciation for the miracle that you are.

As I reflect on the last five years, it would be remiss of me not to mention the importance of having the right people around you. People that will support you on your journey and bring light to your life. Standing at the sidelines and cheering you on! I have been blessed with such incredible people. I call them Earth Angels – though they probably don't know it! Some have walked alongside me for the entirety and some only for a time. My soul family and spiritual running buddies have been a guiding light through the darkest moments and bring immense joy to life. The more in alignment to your true self you become, the more you will open to making these connections and finding your 'tribe'.

There are some absolute fundamentals that I could not have done this without, some of which I have eluded to here and form part of my Alignment Toolkit. Some are an integrated part of my life, others I come back to as needed. They facilitate an ever-deepening connection and awareness, continuous re-alignment and transformation. They keep me centred and grounded, providing an anchor to return to time and time again.

It is this Alignment Toolkit that I now share with clients. It is my vision that every person who feels called, has the knowledge, tools and techniques to create *their* version of an aligned life – physically, mentally, emotionally and spiritually. In doing so, in connecting fully to yourself and what your body needs, it is my experience that radical healing and prevention is possible.

The potent combination of radical self-care, energy alignment and embodied movement facilitates living a life of joy and vitality. The answers *are* inside each of us. But sometimes we need a little help to find them. I see this toolkit, when used with the right intention and the right support, as facilitating access to the answers within and the healing potential they hold.

Your body contains so much wisdom. Everything you have ever experienced is stored within. Sadly, today's modern world pulls us constantly up into our heads. Thinking, doing, busying, pushing, striving. Focused on the incessant external flow of information. A treadmill of distraction. Living this way, disconnected from our emotions, our bodies, we miss the messages we are being sent. Those early warning signals – the whispers "something is wrong".

In making a commitment to Self, to re-connect and build awareness, to listen (I mean *really* listen on the inside, with acceptance and self-compassion), the journey of de-conditioning, de-programming, un-doing, healing, transforming, empowering and growing into who you came here to be can unfold.

In the words of Paulo Coelho - "Maybe the journey isn't so much about becoming anything. Maybe it's about un-becoming everything that isn't really you, so you can be who you were meant to be in the first place".

In taking this approach, learning and applying the tools and techniques that facilitate this process, the potential for healing and transformation is immense. The emotional origins underneath illness and dis-ease cannot be underestimated. I have seen this not only in my own recovery from burnout, depression and anxiety, but also in the people I have supported with this work - with a range of diagnoses including musculoskeletal issues, cancer and auto-immune diseases.

What is contained here is not the promise of a cure or a recommendation to move away from allopathic medicine. Merely an invitation to consider an integrated approach that looks at all levels – physical, mental, emotional and spiritual.

This is all part of the human experience. The dark and the light. The down and the up. The ebbs and the flows. With each stage of our unique journey, we learn something new. We apply it. We course correct and so the cycle continues.

In this interconnected Universe there is an order to all things. A meaning behind *everything*, no matter how chaotic and random it may seem. The signs are there, within and around you all the time – not least in all aspects of your health.

In coming to this place of self-connection; bringing aware-ness and compassion to all that you are holding; *you* have the power to re-align and transform on all levels. You have the power to help yourself *heal* better.

The potential you have at your fingertips to live fully, with meaning and freedom, vitality and joy, is phenomenal. It starts by meeting yourself exactly where you are, with accep-tance and compassion, right now in this moment. And the next moment. And the moment after that. Gather the people that lift you up, the tools and techniques that call to you and apply them time and time again. Practice radical self-care. Make *your* alignment *your* top priority. The hardest part is taking the first step. But, if you do, you'll never regret it. You are worth nothing less, simply by virtue of being here. Nothing less than living the most authentic, joyful, miracu-lous and vibrant life.

ABOUT THE AUTHOR

CARLI THORPE

Carli Thorpe is an Intuitive Alignment Practitioner. She empowers those trapped and burnt out in high pressured work environments by guiding them on a journey. Focusing on self-connection, awareness, alignment and transformation, she guides them to living an aligned life with vitality and joy.

Before starting Vitality Naturally Holistic, Carli spent 15 years in the corporate, public and education sectors managing high profile projects. This meant first-hand experience of the toll this can take on mental, physical and emotional health. She now teaches others the powerful tools, techniques and knowledge (the 'Alignment Toolkit') needed to take back control of their wellbeing, ignite their energy and re-discover their sense of Self.

Carli loves trees, dancing and dark chocolate. She is available for workshops, events and one-to-one coaching and mentoring.

You can reach Carli at:

Email: info@vitalitynaturally.co.uk
Website: www.vitalitynaturally.co.uk

facebook.com/VitalityNaturallyLife
instagram.com/vitalitynaturally
linkedin.com/in/vitalitynaturallyholistic

THERE SHE GLOWS

CATHERINE DODD

I was numb from the waist after a disc ruptured in my back. I had been told I may not be able to have children. As I laid in the hospital bed following an extremely serious back operation I was told I would need a back brace, morphine & would feel like I had been "beaten with a baseball bat" I decided in that moment that I may not have my body right now but I did have my mind....my spirit..... so there it began

It was in those most uncertain days that I decided "I" got to take charge of my life.

I thanked the surgeon and nurses for their care......and in spite of the protocol of needing a back brace and morphine I walked out with nothing stronger than a paracetamol

Was I scared YES! Did I have a clue how it was going to pan out? No

I had been a successful massage and holistic therapist in stunning spas in London (and some not so stunning ones too, just to keep it real). I was told I would need a new career as my physical work would be too much for me.

I was 27, devastated. I had to move back in with my parents on the Isle of Wight, not quite what I had planned.

I had no idea "how" to really change my life but I knew I had my holistic knowledge so I knew I had to dig deep within myself.

Funny how life guides you...even when you think it isn't....what I learnt deeply is that you have everything, all the answers inside of you.

Today and 50,000 plus client contact hours later I work as a movement teacher, Positive Psychology coach and Energy Alignment Mentor.

Pre op I had dallied with working for myself but had always ended up working for others. Looking back I think I believed you had to work hard for your income, I was a real pusher, working until I literally broke my body

I don't think I realised until a lot later just how many of us run that "programme" of rescuing others and validating ourselves through others eyes.

At the pinnacle of push I had 4 jobs. I have very fond memories of working in a rugby cafe in Twickenham, the home of England rugby...that was where my love of rugby really started to those that know me and my how my eyes light up when rugby...or rugby players are mentioned, which I of course put down to the love of the physicality of the game and it being linked to my job..ahem.

I would start at the cafe at 9, finish at 2 then dash for the train to London. I would change into my therapist uniform, change persona into the calm, extremely professional woman who provided an array of world class treatments to celebrities and the uber wealthy where I had a lot of request clients, which created a lot of juggling as there are only so many hours in the day, but I of course "got off" on the validation of being needed. It took me a long time to realise I was actually creating co dependence between myself and my clients. It wasn't until I was learning to be a coach that I had an "aha2 moment around just how much I made myself "needed".

I actually believed I could "fix" people, how ironic seeing as I had a pattern of burn out that went on way before the back operation that it resulted in.

Once finished at 7pm at the salon I would change again, jump on the bus up the High road and arrive by 7.30 to pull pints in a working men's club until midnight.

Yes I certainly did see the whole spectrum of life. Looking back I truly see all our life experiences may happen for a reason or become great teachings that allow us to polish our human "act".

When I moved back to the isle of Wight with my parents I did pretty much the same as above but add in opening my own salon this time & working at my local further education college. I hoped I could make a difference to 16-18 year olds as well as adult learners who wanted to change or start their career in beauty, spa, health & wellbeing

Cue more burn out, a huge realisation that not everyone that attended learning actually wanted a shining career & were perhaps just whiling away time...much to my amazement and frustration, again I thought I could rescue them.

So here I happily was in a career that I loved, I had now (in my eyes) "done good". I'd come back from a life changing surgery back into the industry I was told I mustn't return to.

I had absolutely no idea I was pushing my physical, emotional and energetic body to the brink

Whether it's because I'm a Virgo, seeing my parents be self employed or something completely different I took myself very seriously. It was incredibly important to me to "turn up", to be professional. I did it very well. Can you relate to this? Do you ever put yourself under this pressure?

The thing is being professional is wonderful but it made me so rigid, so stiff, so immoveable....notice those words? That's exactly how I felt in my body. My thoughts were the same- I couldn't do change in any form, my energy was dropping, a little more on that later and before long my health was suffering again, only this time...everywhere.

I suffered with my digestion, my immune system, my mood, and my joints, as soon as I finished work I spent most days off asleep, just trying to catch up.

I started not going out as it took too much energy, yet we need downtime and connection, laughs, pleasure for our wellbeing. I was all about work. I felt extreme guilt when friends that had children laughed at my exhausted story so I didn't mention it.

I had started feeling like a failure as a human being.....not that you would ever know as I did a first rate job at stuffing it down, over compensating by being not just the funny friend, the hilarious friend who, whilst didn't have children, spun many differing plates to try and make up for what I perceived as being the runt of the litter.....at 4'11" I literally did struggle to keep up, yet I used to say I was 6 foot on the inside. I knew for as long as I could remember my passion was to help, support and show others how great their life could be. I grew up in the 90's watching incredibly motivating life coaches break into everyday life, giving us permission to reach for our full potential.... I loved that idea of possibility for as long as I can remember

It started becoming a problem. Creating a duality within myself....I mean I worked in pubs whilst dreaming of speaking on stages, helping masses. People like me didn't do that, yet my parents, my friends were fully supportive.

My job in the wellbeing industry taught me so much is possible. I ferociously studied every therapy going, I was insatiable. Every day was a school day.

The one thing I am never short of in life is enthusiasm.....and stubbornness....both of those qualities have helped me in tough times but actually they can be very restrictive. It wasn't until later when I learnt about our values that I could see a double edged sword here.

My enthusiasm meant I took on everything, because I love life.....then didn't always implement well, equalling a poor result, leading to yet more "runt of the litter" feelings

The stubbornness, whilst amazing for tough challenges meant I could stubbornly fail and not see when to change tact.

I completely believed that I would go through the brick wall, under it over it, around, whatever but I would keep pushing to get the result I wanted....regardless of whether it was actually right me, my soul, my life. In fact I don't even think I was aware that I was "allowed" to live life my way but rather I thought I just had to work hard.

I now realise thanks my eastern teachings that my energy was scattered....

If you asked me where this push energy came from I honestly couldn't pin it down but rather a "just wanting to be liked" persona developed over time, we did move around a fair bit. I grew up in self employment, mainly hospitality, so maybe it developed from there.

I do remember trying to fit in at school each time we moved. By high school I was a very anxious kid, some pretty challenging early life stuff meant I was very fearful. By the time my mock exams arrived I had a huge meltdown in the exam hall......that was the end of school for me. I did exams at home and whilst my friends were out being teenagers I couldn't get past the front door, which of course not many of my peers understood, slowly the offers of going out dried up as they couldn't understand why I couldn't function "normally" Eventually in my teens I was diagnosed with something called Epstein Barr Virus which I now understand to be a stress virus similar to chronic fatigue, I never really understood this until much later in my therapy but I do believe this contributed greatly to the push energy as it affects those "A" type folks, those who push on through emotional as well as physical pain & are not always in connection with themselves due to feeling guilt around sowing down or not achieving their own high standards or what they perceive society expects of them, the irony being your energy is taken so much you can barely do a thing.

I continued to work like a Trojan and burn out, causing panic, fatigue, feelings of shame at my situation when I felt I "should" be getting my sh*t together Catherine.

I don't doubt for a moment that you too have had feelings similar, as I grew from just physical therapy into mindset work and coaching it was a huge light bulb moment around "perception"- the way we perceive our life and how it should be alongside us perceiving that every other person on the planet has got their sh*t together.

 I think we can all burn those unhelpful beliefs down right now if we haven't already. One the most liberating things I did was give myself permission to be me, exactly where I am, have you had that "aha" moment yet too?

So let's talk the duality of stubbornness. I believed that not giving in or up was a spectacular attribute...which it is if you're being chased down the high street by an escaped Tiger but not so much if you become a little blinkered ie you're on your knees tired, you work through illness, you struggle to say no, you offer to go over and above...sound familiar? And how does that serve us exactly?

Yes we are indeed built for good stress aka hormetic stress...as in a little does you good, expands the body and mind beyond its capabilities but as we all know in the modern world sustained busyness isn't so hot. I cannot even begin to tell you the busy/ stress levels I see in my clients daily. It would seem sometimes the more corporate or successful they are, the more need to experience pain as a badge of honour.

How many times do you hear yourself or people you know talk about "pushing" on through something with almost a ton of pride? I used to see this in my male clients a lot but these days I see it in everyone, even kids as the world has become more accessible and busy.

By the time I was forty, health was in decline, I had some very unhealthy boundaries, no social life.I knew there was more for me in life surely but had developed beliefs of shame that I was useless, the runt of the litter. Every time I went for some kind of self help session I would be told I was extremely hard on myself and I had no self esteem.

I'd spent my life propping up that push badge of honour. I was doing all the things such as learning at light speed, going to yoga/ meditation, drinking the green juice, everything short of wearing designer leisure gear and if I'd had the money would have done that too! However because I kept burning out and was single my income was unstable to say the least. Now my badge of honour was starting to become unstable too, not to mention glossy magazines and social media reminding me I hadn't married, or ever had a house, or kids, I was dismal at blending my work and social life, spent weekends asleep and eating chocolate. I felt more like a certain single film character crying into her wine, whilst singing than ever before.

The catalyst really came when I came to do my coaching work, I'd spent years performing physical therapy for clients injuries, Working with athletes that were therapists too meant many of us wore that badge of honour where we worked hard, played hard and as a result had a lot of chiropractic/osteopathy treatment to offset it....perhaps justify it.

Now though I was entering a field of energy and mindset where you TRULY had to walk you talk

At the age of 40 with beliefs and perceptions that I should be way ahead, a chip on my shoulder about working hard and "you'll do well" belief, whilst proving the complete opposite. A passion to help and transform people from their own dire depths into the kind of success story you see in the films whilst stubbornly failing and continuing to fail myself. All whilst a ten year relationship had ended at that point too leaving me in full victim, woe is me mode. Shouting at the universe for a solution whilst actually and brutally honestly getting stubborn about doing the real work of change, which means coming out of your comfort zone. Taking real action, embodying the uncomfortable parts of you that no one in school or college, or in fact anywhere tells you that is in fact what is required at this point.

I had to take that awkward, vulnerable, not liking what I was seeing or being long hard look at my life.....it was at that moment I realised that perhaps what people were saying about me being hard on myself & lacking self esteem was in fact true as I berated myself time and time again for the perceived "state of my life"

The utter irony that I could literally support anyone in changing their world and do it with my eyes shut, it was an absolute gift of mine, yet how the hell had I got to this point of not doing it for myself.....

At that moment I do believe I heard the chink of armour fall away, the "badge of push" energy clatter to the floor beside me very loudly, causing me to feel like I'd just stood naked in the centre of the pitch at my beloved Twickenham stadium with vulnerability.

I don't know if you've yet felt it but there is nothing quite like you getting real, raw and hugely honest with yourself. You may well squirm in discomfort but I truly believe it is the best option moving forward, said with Virgo logic, a wry smile and a dollop of humour, because I know what getting vulnerable with yourself feels like.

I can't say I had a plan about how I was going to pull it all together like a Mum given world book day dress up costume details at 8.55 but what followed next was nothing short of miraculous. If ever I had doubted the whole universe has your back thing (though not going to lie i did try!) I was well & truly proven wrong. THE UNIVERSE REALLY DOES HAVE YOUR BACK

My life was in mid life tatters, I had nothing to lose, yet all the fears that were stopping me making it happen. At that point the realisation that our thoughts & beliefs shape our world rang so loudly, well in fact they literally rang in the form of my phone.

It was a coaching friend who told me they were just starting this new "thing" & would I be interested, as I stared out of my salon window into the autumn rain lashing down from grey skies something in me said yes, do the thing...that moment was the start of my coaching career. Little did I realise the journey of transforming one's life is one of "you get out what you put in".

I completed a 10 month intensive coaching experience before I was even able to move onto the coaching certification to make sure I could support my clients without my own stuff getting in the way. Every belief, judgement and opinion I had ever held was called before the highest energy...universal. Not only did I become a coach, I became a titanium one that calls our mind, body & energy into alignment

I went from life changing surgery to patterns of burn out, push energy that declined my health and lost me work, seeking validation, rescuing others, lacking self esteem, wanting to remain comfortable, invisible even in my business

to becoming a mind, body and energy coach, it sounds so cliché yet it is my truth.

However I am never going to sit here and say it happened over night. I'm also going to say it felt like I had no idea what I was doing, I longed for this transformation to look like "others"...see that comparisonitis pattern creeping in there too!

I so wanted it to look glossy, for me to take a metaphorical bow, to feel like a swan gliding into my new life position right on cue...when the reality was I stumbled like a comedian on to the stage of life, forgetting my lines, wondering what to say to my awaiting audience and hoping no one noticed I was a fraud. I cringed at my arrival that was as awkward as a teenager in the school play BUT I was trying, I was doing it.

I can remember my early forays into announcing I'd be coaching and mentoring on social media. Actually trying to casually mention the fact I was doing a rather huge new arm to my business that came from my own life mess, I laugh as I write this now as I now teach coaches and mentors.... it is still truly one of those "pinch my arm, is this real" moments.

So the coaching and mentoring modality that I mainly use is an incredible system called the Energy Alignment Method. It is has its roots in Chinese medicine, which dovetails perfectly with my breathwork, Qi Gong for health mindful movement teaching, NLP, positive psychology & law of attraction with a super power of Kinesiology on the side, this is the bit for me that got my attention....I was already a Kinesiologist (using muscle testing to work with specific health issues). I knew the power we hold in our bio feedback system, think of it like this we know we have a physical self, we can touch it and see it in a mirror, yet in the west we don't recognise the power of working with our "Qi" think of this as life force energy, the mystical power that illuminates us from the moment of conception.

Many different cultures in the east see this as our energy body, infinitely linked to a greater energy than us. You may have heard of it in the west as an "aura" so it dropped in to me that it's like electricity, we can't see it yet we know it's there as we flick the switch and it lights our home, we are the same. When we recognise that the power lays within us it is a game changer.

So this modality uses our body as the muscle test with a sway which bypasses our conscious thinking.

I see so many clients and myself "then" looking for answers to their life woes in their brain only energy, saying things like "I know I should do that" then taking absolutely no action. I "know" it's this thing that caused that belief....in reality that is just a clever subterfuge for us to bring some kind of figuring out energy to our situation. The trouble with that is it can become a story we lean on, remember my story with the push energy being the "badge of honour" because I believed in order to have a good life you had to work crazy hours?

We actually have 3 brains our head, our heart and what we call in the east our Hara, in the west we know it as our belly or gut instinct. We may not have access to an energy alignment practitioner immediately what we can do is ask ourselves powerful questions and journal around the issues to see what we can glean to move us forward & take action.

It's easy for us to "logic it out" however let's give ourselves permission (huge tip number two btw!) to drop into our heart and then ask again.

I quite often ask my clients to put their hand on their heart as we work together, to really feel into the power of the question they are asking themselves & of course followed by what action can we take to get a step closer to our desire, the Hara part of our 3 treasures of head, heart, hara

As I mentioned in that past paragraph we are tend to be great at supporting others, really gentle but are we that permissive and gentle with ourselves too?

Let's really grow compassion for ourselves as well as others

Now the biggest thing for me, you heard me mention earlier that the universe has your back, what I want to mention here as it was such a big "aha" is that we are the same, that Qi, higher wisdom, is you.

I have seen so many people take course after course seeking answers or spending hours in talking therapies churning up the past, of course for some this is correct protocol however my biggest finding is that it comes back to you, choice, action taking, even if small AND the realisation that we don't need fixing. There is absolutely nothing wrong with us, we are always learning and exactly where we need to be at exactly the right time, feel into the energy of that, can you feel the relief of giving yourself that realisation?

Lastly & important to us pushers is how often are you truly embodying the work, it's when life is at its busiest and most challenging that's REALLY when we must take the time for us

These days I help people marry up their mind, body and energy with coaching work and classes. I'm extremely lucky to receive feedback everyday from clients that recognise a daily practice self compassion and self enquiry helps them to manage their stress levels, communicate better so improving their relationships, truly hearing their body when asked for rest, instead of shouting at it or thrashing it further.

A huge part of change for me is daily, incremental practice such as -

Listening to the words you use with your self- if you wouldn't say them to a friend then sure as heck don't use them to yourself, the biggest relationship you are EVER going to have is with yourself so let it be a harmonious one!

When you hear yourself say you don't have time-THAT is the exact moment you stop, even if for a few moments to take some deep breath, we know it helps us, what we don't often realise is when done regularly a cumulative effect takes place in the nervous system. ALL of your body's systems stand down, shifting into rest and digest, the parasympathetic part of the nervous system that helps us to heal is like exercise- it doesn't have to be much to have a very noticeable difference on our mind, body & energy, giving us a chance to view life through a much healthier lens, creating far more resilience and tolerance to life

I have been told I should be on prescription more than once and have been lucky enough to take my work to doctors and hospitals.....so you never know!

What has changed in me? Well instead of feeling like "the runt of the litter" I look back and think wow how much has changed, I would never thrash myself in that way ever again and in spite of being 4'11 I regularly get called a powerhouse or a dynamo. It's fair to say the lady that was is very long gone and in her place the invisible day dreamer has and continues to become (because we always learning right?) a reluctant, hesitant then finally an embodied leader able to not only guide herself but others through this thing called life that let's face it is up and down like a certain suspension bridge in London!

You don't know what you don't know- the unconscious incompetence coaching model. I had absolutely no idea my life could be this level of good and beyond. I can to give myself the permission to grow into each new level.

I now KNOW I have embodied my work, if you can call your life's passion work, into a flow that totally fits me and I'm very pleased to say my health! I of course continue to learn, evolve and embody daily through life's challenges with more wisdom

Only working with clients that are a complete fit, for us both....I have found the best magic comes from that combination

Only working when I choose to with zero guilt or need to rescue, that's when I knew things had really changed, no more dashing about, even in a pandemic-my way always!

~

AS my chapter of this enlightening book comes to a close I would love to make you a promise in this moment that will see you good for many years to come

Invest in YOU, I'm not just talking money, we have been programmed time and time again by society, relationships and our self over decades. We would never forget to put petrol in our car as we wouldn't get to our intended destination. We would never not put oil & water in its engine as we know it would seize & be the end of our car, we would never not build a boundary fence around our property to keep it safe and secure. We would never not charge our phone as we recognise the vital functions that it gives us alongside the ability to communicate with the world...you get where I'm going with this

Prioritise YOU, yes it may take a 180 degree turn, a bit of time and effort to change habits but that's exactly what they are programmes, habits, beliefs about our self. As such they are completely re writable, contrary to belief it doesn't have to be hard, you really do get out what you put in...Remember it's when life blows the hardest that we need to secure those fences of ours...and it can be done in a matter of minutes, we don't have to do it all at once!

I am so grateful to you for taking the time to wander through my contribution to this transformational space. I hope you feel the loving kindness bestowed within these words, may they land in your heart and guide you gently through YOUR life

If you would love to share space please do come on over to Facebook, I'm Catherine Page on there, or email me at catherinedodd@live.co.uk

Wishing you well.

ABOUT THE AUTHOR

CATHERINE DODD

Catherine Dodd is a Positive Psychology Coach & Energy Alignment Method master mentor, 200 Hour Qi Gong instructor and Breath work facilitator who helps business owners, CEO's, coaches and leaders grow their health and wellbeing so they can continue to impact and grow their audience with thriving energy whilst living a life they love.

Catherine has 30 years experience and over 50,000 client contact hours within health, wellbeing, spa, teaching and coaching. She has worked in 5 star establishments, the leisure industry and has taught in further education. She helps business owners thrive in wellbeing, energy and health so they can continue to create wealth and live their purpose with more ease.

Catherine is a passionate wellbeing advocate blending eastern and western approaches in her down time and loves spending time at her local beach and finding calm in nature.

Catherine is available for corporate wellbeing sessions and speaking engagements as well as wellbeing and coaching programmes

You can reach Catherine at

Email- catherinedodd@live.co.uk

facebook.com/Catherine%20Page
instagram.com/soul_spa_success
linkedin.com/in/Catherine%20Dodd

SOUL SEARCHER

> *"What you think you create. What you feel you attract. What you imagine you become."*

Buddha

fter 10 years in corporate, I knew I had to get out. Nothing I found myself doing in my professional life resonated one bit with the whisperings of my soul. I was earning far more than most of my peers and in senior positions in the companies I worked for. But it wasn't enough. I was seriously out of alignment, and I knew it. I had to do something. But was I just going to throw it all away? And for what? What was I going to do instead? I had no answers. I just knew that living a lie was no longer an option and that I owed it to myself to honour the deep-yearning within and step into my authentic-self. I deliberated significantly over the next 5 years as I challenged myself to overcome my fears, let go of the past and commit fully to pursuing my passions.

Finally, 15 years after starting my corporate career, I quit. I was free at long last.

Almost 20 years on from the start of my career and no longer bound by the shackles of the corporate world, I've found my truth and the freedom to live life in line with my highest vision. The values I live by every day are my own not those of some organisation or product I don't believe in or resonate with. As a Master Energy Alchemy & Intuitive Life Coach, Meditation Teacher and Reiki Master, I live life in line with my desire to be of service to humanity. To be able to deeply impact others by helping them on their journey, and to have others thank you from the bottom of their hearts for having changed their lives, is all the reward I need. Living life in alignment with my soul feels amazing and I wouldn't have it any other way.

I'd always had a burning desire to dedicate my life to helping others, in fact, it's the one thing I've always been clear about. But in the early days, I lacked a vision, and the courage and wisdom to follow my intuition despite not having the answers. Having been brought up to value academic achievement above everything else, I'd been easily led by the well-intentioned guidance of others to go to university and get a degree. And indeed, not really knowing who my authentic self was, it felt safer to listen to my masculine left-brain and the logical-sounding guidance of those around me as they cheered me towards the academic path.

I spent 4 years studying and obtained a 2-1 Master's in International Business and Languages, followed by another 2 years to obtain a Chartered Institute of Marketing Postgraduate Diploma in Marketing for which I obtained a distinction, coming in the top 3% globally. As a Chartered Marketer I felt at the top of my game. I was now fixated on my next goal of becoming a director. In the business world I became highly successful, but I was a fraud, an imposter, someone who didn't belong, and I knew it.

Admitting this to myself was easy but in the months and years that followed, the battle between my left and right brain ensued. My intuition and right-brain wouldn't let me rest; pushing me to change and urging me break out of my comfort zone. But my logical and analytical left brain kept me stuck in old patterns and cycles, driven by the fear of leaving everything I'd worked so hard for behind. It was this fear that kept me well and firmly rooted in the known despite my mental turmoil.

If I'd known what I do now, I'd have told my younger self "You know when you know". If you feel, deep inside that you're not in alignment, and that feeling isn't just a fleeting impulse, then that's your right brain, your intuition and higher self, letting you know quite clearly that you're not in alignment. It's that simple. There's no need to spend months and years like I did listening to the chattering of your left-brain as it rolls out the red-carpet for every reason under the sun why you should stay within your current, unhappy reality and not honour your soul's calling.

I used to think working harder was the solution to every-thing. There goes my left-brain again! This belief was deeply rooted in my upbringing and society's collective and outdated patriarchal belief that to succeed you just need to work harder. As a youngster I was highly academic, achieving the best grades at school and college. However, as I grew older, I increasingly became tired of working harder at things that didn't excite me and when I reached university, the battle of wills between my left and right brain began.

Choosing a degree was challenging as I'd absolutely no idea what I wanted to do. Careers counselling was focussed on what job you thought you might like to do in future, and I was encouraged down the academic route. I now see this was an incredibly masculine, left-brained approach. I didn't know what I wanted as no one had explored my core desires with me; how I wanted to feel and what lifestyle I envisaged. With little time left to submit university application forms, I approached the problem logically, my then modus operandi. I reasoned that everything in life is business so a business degree would be useful and buy me another 4 years to decide what I did want to do.

I was an avid reader of psychology, spirituality, philosophy, and self-development books. But at that stage in my life, it hadn't occurred to me that personal interests could become your life-long passion and work. To me what you did for enjoyment was separate and outside of 'working hard'. And studying was all about working hard. And so it was that I ended up taking a Master's in International Business and Spanish. As I reflect on it now, I can see that although I didn't know it at the time, I was settling for less. By compart-mentalising work and pleasure, I was creating an unhealthy rod for my own back where I'd forever be dissatisfied by a career which symbolised working hard for financial reward rather than doing something I truly enjoyed.

During university I began delving into spirituality. I visited the local Buddhist Centre, attending meditation and

Buddhist philosophy workshops. I also read voraciously around the subject; deep diving into anything I could get my hands on. Reflecting on it now, I see I put much more energy into, and read more widely around, my personal interests than my degree. Choosing between the meaning of life, consciousness, and self-development on the one hand and finance, economics and accountancy on the other was a no-brainer.

After my second year, having dedicated myself very little to academic study, my tutor threatened to boot me out if my grades didn't improve. That summer, whilst everyone else was enjoying the sun, I employed old faithful 'working harder' and studied till the cows came home. And my efforts paid off, I passed my retakes with flying colours. Through this I learnt that if I'm not really interested in something, I don't want to do it and it won't be enjoyable. I also learnt that if I really want something, then if I set my mind to it, I can achieve anything, even if it's maths which doesn't come easily to me and certainly doesn't light me up.

And so, I continued in my misalignment, spending my third year in Spain, partying and at the beach when I was supposed to be at Spanish university. As a British-Ecuadorian, I'd been brought up English-Spanish bilingual, so it came easily to bunk class and still get top grades. At the time I didn't stop to ask why I was resisting my studies, and it certainly didn't cross my mind that it was unhealthy since I'd convinced myself that work and pleasure were separate. Back in the UK, I worked hard in my final year to get the degree result I wanted, regardless of how I felt deep down.

I now see how unhealthy this inflexibility was, keeping me bound to completing a course I had no affinity with. Not finishing would have felt like a failure but I see now that the real failure was not connecting with how I was feeling inside. The ambivalence I felt towards my studies reflected the discord I felt within. At graduation, I felt a strange mixture of achievement – for making my family proud and for having proved to myself that I have a dogged determination second to none! – coupled with a strange emptiness.

That summer I buried myself in self-development books and experienced the first of many spiritual awakenings. The awakening was a dark but enlightening and liberating experience which caused me to question the very foundations of reality. It was the first time I'd consciously experienced the fight between duality in my own being; the darkness of the ego versus the lightness of spirit and the vibration of oneness and love. Spilling over with joy and elation, I shared my deepest discoveries with anyone who'd listen. But my revelations were at best met with suspicion or at worst dismissed as the ramblings of a lunatic.

I felt completely misunderstood. Never in my life before or since have I felt so completely alone. I'd finally connected with spirit, my soul and the light and it smiled back at me with unconditional love. I'd connected with the infinite, life-giving intelligence which created us, the universe and everything in it, and it was joyous and uplifting. I'd found the meaning which had for so long been missing in my life, but I was being denied the authenticity of my experience by those around me. I expressed my interest in coaching to share my new-found enlightenment with others as well as my desire to travel to India to study Buddhist meditation. I was met with disbelief and ridicule. I began questioning myself. Maybe I'd completely lost it. Looking back, I see that the violent awakening was a desperate attempt by my soul to wake me up from the denial I was in. But the scare it gave me, to the point of questioning my own sanity, coupled with the logical reasoning of those around me to pursue a graduate job kept me bound on the path of misalignment.

My first job was at a global company listed on the stock exchange. From there I went on to work for other global businesses. The lifestyle was glamorous; international business class flights, limo and chauffer service, 5-star hotels, swanky restaurants and generally living a life of luxury in parallel to working like a dog! I appeared as an expert on breakfast TV, addressed hundreds at conferences and met with government officials, Ministers and top business leaders. As my career progressed, I occupied positions of greater seniority, my salary rose exponentially, as did the shares I'd been awarded for high and exceptional performance. I was on the path to becoming a director by age 30. With all this what was the problem? Well, whilst this was exciting and fun for a fresh-faced 23-year-old, the shine quickly wore off. None of it resonated with me and something was missing.

I pushed hard for results whilst simultaneously neglecting my wellbeing. I felt stressed and the cracks began showing. Tension in my head, neck and shoulders was mounting from excessively long hours on my laptop and I was struggling to relax and sleep; my brain on overdrive from the infinite to do list. In the evening I'd flick on the TV for some escapism only to find that my mind was elsewhere - on a business report, a customer meeting or anywhere else work-related - just not at home, relaxing. Similarly, at night I'd lie in bed with my to-do-list circulating like a merry-go-round for hours. "This is no way to live" I told myself "Something's got to give".

I'd dabbled in meditation at university and had the perception that it could help me switch off. I'd seen pictures of people meditating serenely on beaches, forests and mountains and the peacefulness in the images seemed like the idyllic escape I needed from my frenetic lifestyle. I enrolled on a course at the local Buddhist Centre. It wasn't what I expected, and I became frustrated by the incessant chatter of my mind. It would be years later, after completing my Meditation Teacher Training, that I'd really click with the practice and embedded it as a daily ritual. But back then, my practice was sporadic, frustrating, and misguided. I approached it like everything else I had in life, striving to achieve rather than allowing myself to experience the fullness of my being without judgement and expectation. But the small breakthroughs, glimpses of inner peace and the fact that it was slowly helping me to train my mind to direct attention where I wanted rather that have my mind control me, motivated me to persist.

We're taught our whole lives to do and achieve. Yet meditation is the art of non-doing. Allowing yourself to observe and to be. Whatever you find in that moment; tired, energetic, stressed, peaceful, sad, joyful and every other thought, feeling and sensation within the spectrum of our human experience. We're taught to judge experiences as good or bad rather than observe shades of grey; an unhealthy duality leading us to crave what we like and be averse to what we don't. Medita-tion teaches us to observe ourselves, our environment, and others, let go of judgement and approach our practice and lives with greater openness, patience, compassion, and acceptance. Learning to cultivate these qualities increasingly brought more balance and discipline to my mind. As time went on, I saw everything around me with greater clarity. I began coming to terms with the fact that I wanted out of corporate and terrifyingly began facing my fears.

I remember reading 'The Element: How Finding Your Passion Changes Everything' by Ken Robinson. The book explores the failings of our current education system to nurture students' natural talents regardless of whether we think they're 'academic enough'. He features geniuses such as Matt Groening (creator of the Simpsons) whose school reports noted he'd amount to nothing because he was disrup-tive, drawing cartoons rather than knuckling down. Matt went on to great things. He felt so passionately about his creativity that he put it first, regardless of what others thought. I found the stories inspirational; a reminder that we don't need to fit into a box and that connecting with your passion is the most important thing in life. But how do you find your passion? And do you find it, or does it find you? There seemed to be a few lucky souls who had been gifted with this insight from birth or early childhood. But I didn't have that clarity and despite soul-searching and praying to the universe for answers, I wasn't any clearer. On reflection, I can see that the universe was giving me what I was putting out. I was waiting for the answer, so the universe responded by waiting. The realisation dawned on me that if I continued to wait, I could reach the end of my life still waiting.

In parallel, I was searching for meaning. I'd given myself a scare during my first spiritual awakening, so I'd put my soul-searching in a box and thrown away the key. But in my late 20s, I became increasingly aware that something was missing. And so, after years of avoiding anything spiritual, I began exploring the part of my life that felt most meaningful. In addition to lighting up my soul, I hoped that my pursuits would give me the clarity I needed on what to dedicate my life to. I began looking into Meditation Teacher and Reiki Master training. I was hesitant at first given the investment required but told myself in that if I didn't try out new things I'd maybe never find out where my passions lay. And so, justifying this as an investment in my soul and granting myself permission to spend money on my mission of finding meaning and purpose in my life, I bit the bullet and joined the course. A few years later, I was a qualified Meditation Teacher, Reiki Master, and member of the Complementary Medical Association.

Working with my first clients was awesome and challenged my assumption that work and pleasure were separate. I'd taken action to change the course of my future and was no longer waiting. The universe responded instantly. As soon as I started shining my light, sharing my gifts with those around me, the magic happened. The universe reflects our truth back to us like a mirror. When we acknowledge our gifts and live life in line with our authentic selves, expressing those gifts in service to others, the Law of Attraction draws like-to-like. I received numerous emails from clients thanking me from the bottom of their hearts for profoundly changing their lives. Serving another beautiful soul in this way is the best feeling in the world. I felt I was living in line with my soul's purpose to help others learn and grow on their journey in this lifetime. I became more comfortable following my intuition; acknowledging that if I followed the things I loved, I'd find joy. I realised that the path to honouring your soul's calling is a life-long journey. By doing what you love you uncover the truth your soul already knows. You don't need to have the answers to everything. What matters is following the gentle whispers of your soul. Everything you need is already inside you. Once you stop looking outside and start looking within, everything falls into place. When you meditate, listening very attentively and patiently without expectation, you'll hear your soul calling you home.

I wasn't at my final destination but was now confident enough to know that for more to reveal itself I had to let go of the past to make way for the new. I read "Feel the fear and do it anyway" by Susan Jeffers PhD. Another pivotal book on my journey which helped give me the courage to break free of past conditioning and jack in my corporate career. I asked myself "What's the worst that could happen if I left to do something else?". The answer was return to corporate business and get a new job. In that moment, I realised I was already living my worst-case scenario! Once I saw the situation this way, suddenly the decision didn't seem so big nor so final. If things didn't work out, I'd be back where I was, in a job I disliked, but at least I'd have tried something new. Of course, it wasn't my intention go back to corporate but just knowing I had the option, gave me the courage to try something else.

On my last day at work, rebelling from my corporate straight jacket, I wore an unconventional snazzy dress, glitter biker boots with tattoos on show and my 'fuck work' badge. I'd never felt so liberated in all my life. I caused quite a stir at the office with some of my team finding it particularly amusing and labelling me a legend. As I made my way home later that day, I felt like I'd just got out of jail. And in some ways, I had. After almost a decade and a half, I'd finally liberated myself from my self-imposed shackles of pretending to be someone I wasn't and doing a job I disliked just for money. I no longer had to grin and bear it. From here on I'd answer only to my soul's calling; doing what I loved. Even though I'd reconciled that I could go back, in that moment I knew I wouldn't. Life would never be the same again.

I began the next phase of my life with what I'd always yearned for, time alone for travel, deep reflection, and solitary spiritual practice. I began planning my long-awaited spiritual pilgrimage, booked my round-the world ticket and hopped on a plane. First stop Peru. Deep in the Amazon jungle, I spent time journeying with the shaman and sacred medicine ayahuasca. I had profound experiences which were joyful and uplifting and cemented my connection with the Divine. I was visited by several spirit animals including a black puma, an archetype which has been with me throughout my life. It reminded me to look within and draw on my inner strength. Before I'd told him anything about myself, the head Shaman had felt into my energy and told me that my aura was pure and vibrationally high and that my mission here on Earth was as a healer. The whole experience was validating and reassuring; I was in communion with the Divine and being thanked for never giving up on my faith despite the violent awakenings I'd had which had led me to question my own sanity. I visited the Earth's sacral chakra at Lake Titicaca. And in the Andean mountains; Machu Picchu, Incan ruins and other spiritually significant sites in the sacred valley, taking part in shamanic heart-healing ceremonies with the sacred San-Pedro medicine.

Next stop New Zealand and the ancient, Māori culture. Incan spirituality had a strong focus on Mother Earth (Pachamama) and Father Cosmos (Waricocha) and the importance of balance between these two cosmic energies: the dark, feminine-Earth energy and light, masculine-Cosmic energy. I would see these themes repeating throughout my journey. There was a strong focus on these centralising energies within nature, the universe and all of creation. I embarked on a solitary retreat to a remote moun-tain hut in the NZ Alps for the winter solstice in sub-zero temperatures. It was basic living. Each day I collected and chopped wood to keep the wood fire burning and stay warm, went on woodland mountain walks, basked in the glory of nature, spent time in deep meditation and read books about ancient Māori spirituality.

Hopping over to Australia, I attended a solitary meditation retreat at the Buddhist De-Tong Ling Retreat Centre. My plan was for 8 hours contemplation per day leaving time in the evening to explore Buddhist texts in the meditation hut. I'd never attempted such long periods of meditation and as the days wore on it became increasingly challenging. Heeding my intuition, I allowed myself the flexibility to meditate less in the final days as my concentration waned. Meditating for such an extended period was challenging but hugely insightful. Moving onto the Red Centre, I delved into ancient aboriginal spirituality and visited the Earth's solar plexus chakra, Uluru. As a Leo my ruling planet is the Sun and by visiting the Uluru, I was honouring the masculine aspects within me alongside my spiritual development goals of opening to my feminine energy.

In Vietnamese temples I learnt about the Âm dương – the harmony between pairs of natural energy forces; fertile Earth (Âm) and the warm sun (dương). Again, the themes of light and dark as basic forces of nature playing out in another ancient, belief system across the other side of the world from other belief systems when there would have been no way of them communicating with each other at the time. To me this congruence points towards a universal truth at the core of everything. That, as Einstein put it, "Everything is energy" and that we are all connected by forces which cannot be seen and understood by the five senses alone. I ended there with a Sivananda Yoga retreat.

In Thailand I attended a highly challenging 10-day silent Buddhist Vipassana retreat. On arrival, we were asked to hand in our worldly possessions; no food, books, electronic devices, crystals, or religious paraphernalia allowed. The practice was strict; 10 hours daily alternating between breathing and body-awareness sitting practices. We'd have short breaks between hourly sessions but other than that were asked to sit completely still without moving, learning to work with the pain and discomfort which inevitably sets in when you sit motionless for extended periods. Character building to say the least!

My next stop was India. I attended Buddhist talks and visited the home of the 14th Dalai Lama, attending one of his discourses. I also spent time in Bodh Gaya home to the Bodhi tree under which the Buddha found enlightenment. Taken under the wing of a Buddhist monk, he handed me a fallen leaf from the Bodhi tree, before leading me by the hand to the sacred tree. I thanked him for the gift and guidance and proceeded to sit in meditation amongst the other pilgrims. I will never forget the energy there; the most magnifying and electric spiritual energy I've experienced anywhere in the world. After visiting many more Hindu, Sikh, and Buddhist temples I finished my time in India with an Ayurveda and Yoga retreat in Rishikesh.

Penultimate stop, Egypt. Here I visited the pyramids and Sphinx, the Earth's throat chakra. I immersed myself in the ancient beliefs of the pharaohs and was struck by the similarities to other ancient cultures. The Sphinx faces East towards the sun God – Ra. It's the Sphinx's adoration for the sun that causes it to rise out of itself, out of the Earth from which it's made, to reach continually for the higher level of it's being, called by the light. I was struck by the parallel to the journey of personal transformation that we as spiritual beings living a human experience undergo as we learn and grow.

Returning to the UK, I end my pilgrimage on the winter solstice at the Earth's heart chakra - Stonehenge, Glastonbury - where I join other like-minded souls and my husband to celebrate our love for the Earth, the cycles of nature, the universe and the Divine. The winter solstice is the point in the year where all ancient cultures come together to celebrate the end of the darkness and welcome in the light. Having celebrated the winter solstice only 6 months before in NZ, the symbolism of welcoming in the light twice in one year wasn't lost on me as I stepped out of the darkness and into my light.

And so here I am 20 years later having gone full circle, having returned to the call from within to pursue my passions of meditation and coaching others on their journey of self-discovery and transformation. It would be easy to look back and beat myself up about things I feel I could have done differently but I wouldn't have learnt what I have had I not had those experiences. I did the best I could knowing what I did at the time. And nothing is ever a waste of energy or time. The universal intelligence at the core of our souls' journey is too clever for that. Everything happens at the perfect time, in the perfect order for the right reasons. It's down to us to reflect deeply, understand the lessons, take the learning, and use it to grow and to flourish. The experiences I've had have helped shape who I am today and given me the depth of personal experience to enable me to better coach and support others on their journey. You're the best teacher you could ever wish for; all you need do is learn how to tune in to the wisdom within.

Step into your truth by becoming more aware of what you truly love and feel passionately about. When you calm the chattering of the thinking mind and tune into your intuition, great things happen. I've seen it time and time again in myself and in my clients; in the beautiful souls I admire and respect for committing to undertake the work on themselves. Fellow soul searchers who aren't afraid to break out of their comfort zone and peel away the layers to uncover another piece of who we truly are. And each time allowing the light within to shine more brightly.

And so here I am living the dream. I don't have all the pieces in place, and I never will. For what kind of dream would it be if it were limited? What I do have is a life being lived, authentically in line with my purpose, values, and truth. I look forward to every day with joy and anticipation knowing that when I wake up, I'll be dedicating myself to my soul's mission doing what I love. And if I don't want to do it, I won't. That's liberation. A life well lived needs to honour its truth. Discover your limiting beliefs and blocks and break those fuckers down! Come out of dark and take off the blinkers. Free yourself from self-imposed shackles and limitation. Go on the greatest adventure of your life; the journey to the depths of your soul and back again to become aware of who you really are and what you're truly capable of. Give yourself the greatest gift of living your life with infinite possibility and pure potentiality.

When you do the work, the universe responds by giving you the clarity and wisdom you need to take the next step. All you need to do is to trust that next step, even if it makes no sense to you at the time. Just go along for the ride. Enjoy the journey. For life isn't about the final destination, it's all about the journey. It's OK to be a work-in-progress. Indeed, that's all we ever will be. And I say that in the fullest sense; for the universe allows for all possibility. Your soul is limitless and infinite. Life is a blank canvass, and you are a masterpiece in the making so go create the life of your dreams.

ABOUT THE AUTHOR

CAZ LANDON

Caz Landon is a Master Energy Alchemy & Intuitive Life Coach, recognised by the International Authority for Professional Coaching & Mentoring (IAPC&M). She is also a qualified Meditation Teacher, Reiki Master and Author. Caz loves to support fellow soul searchers unleash their unique and limitless potential in order to live the life of their dreams.

Before setting up SoulSearcherz™, Caz spent 15-years in senior management positions within different industries.

After a successful corporate career and 20-years' experience coaching teams and individuals, she now offers personal transformation coaching.

Caz supports individuals to release stress, nurture self-love and self-care, set healthy boundaries, transcend limiting beliefs, build confidence, overcome fear, cultivate positive behavioural qualities, tune into intuition and higher self and find what's joyful and meaningful.

When Caz isn't soul searching, she loves travelling, reading and writing, time out in the wild and enjoying the fabulous company of her beautiful husband, family and friends.

Caz is available for coaching, writing and speaking opportunities. Discover more with SoulSearcherz^{TM}:

Website - www.soulsearcherz.com

Email – support@soulsearcherz.com

Facebook Business Page:

https://www.facebook.com/soulsearcherzcommunity

YouTube:

https://www.youtube.com/channel/UCzrP3gU-yh9JMCzhnSaYiIQm

 facebook.com/caz.landon

 instagram.com/cazlandon.soulsearcherz

linkedin.com/in/cazlandon

CUPS OVERFLOWING

KAREN CAREY

INTRODUCTION

You can't pour from an empty cup! I'm a woman, a caregiver, a sister, Daughter, Mom, Grandma, Aunt, and friend. I love to care for others just as I know you do. But we have a huge flaw. We don't care for ourselves as we care for others. So, here's my story and I pray that you will come to care for you first so that you too, can always pour from a cup that is full or filled to overflowing and never have an empty cup.

I was that young mom, wife, working full-time and had no idea what the heck I was doing. I knew in my mind I was career driven, but also wanted a family, wanted to be a mom, a good mom and wife. I dove in with both feet. Forty plus hours a week at my job, then home to care for a newborn, home, and husband. I was doing it all, but I was exhausted. From one task to the next. Diapers (yes, I did the cloth diapers), bottles, laundry, cleaning, groceries, work, husband. I had no energy. I felt run down. No desire to do much else. What happened to me? Not saying I wasn't happy, I was just feeling empty, and drained. There was no time for me, for the things I use to do. I needed change, but wasn't sure how? What do I do? What would I do? How do I change this?

Years later I returned to college to get my nursing degree. Children, yes two of them, now 5 and 10 years old (and a 17-year-old stepson). Then, years later, I was that mom with now 2 full-time children, 5 years apart and a part-timer that was with us for all holidays and summertime.

Fast forward some years, the kids were in high school, and middle school. Lord help me, they were non-stop. He was in Football, Basketball, and Lacrosse; she was in cheerleading, softball, and youth group. I was the taxi driver, cheerleading coach, and football team nurse. I was working full-time nights so that I was there for all of their events, and games, housework, cooking, cleaning, laundry (oh, they were old enough to do their own laundry), groceries, and summer youth mission trips. Craziness, yes it was! Oh, and by the way, I was singing in a choir, and connecting with women at our church. Tired, yes, I was! Enjoying my children, definitely! In need of some down time? Yes! But how? When? Where and how would that fit into this equation? I was concerned about so much. I saw weight gain; this was due to terrible eating habits. I was not sleeping well, I was working nights, so I slept maybe 5 hours before I was up and out. I knew this is not good, and things needed to change. Ok, I thought, I would at some point, maybe? Does this sound remotely familiar?

My son had graduated from high school, and moved on to college, and work; daughter was in high school, and was still cheerleading. I was still the football team nurse and worked dayshift. I was still a youth sponsor with my daughter, and my singing continued. I was leading women's bible study/circle group, along with all the at home stuff. Also, as the nurse in the family, everyone came to me for aches, pangs, pains, looking to me for "diagnoses". I was not a doctor, I didn't and couldn't diagnose anything, but they thought that I could.

I was so tired. I needed a break. I needed some relief. I was not feeling great, still. What was 'not feeling so great'? I was tired, overweight. I had some pounds that I needed to get rid of. I was feeling muscle aches mainly in my joints because of the weight. Pain in my back and shoulders because that is where I carried my stress. I was consistently getting sinus infections. That was my compromised immune system due to lack of sleep, and stress. So, just not feeling the way that I knew I should be feeling. Ever felt that way, and had no plan on how to change things, how to make YOU better? That is what I was feeling, and what I needed.

During the next phase of my life, things were constantly changing. At this point, the children were adults, thank you Jesus! I transitioned from being a busy mom, to being director of women's ministries at our church. I was now on the worship team, and still singing with the choir, an acapella group, working full time, caring for a sick grandmother, dealing with aging parents, and a sister with an undiagnosed illness. I had parents that had knee replacements, and hospitalizations. I was the medical power-of-attorney for them, and had to step into that role when things weren't being handled properly with their health care.

As a nurse, I have worked Critical Care (Cardiac ICU), Labor & Delivery, Operating Room, Administrator of Surgery Center & Urology Practice, Transitional Care Coordinator for Home Health and Delegating Nurse for Mentally Disabled Adults. Being that nurse who has worked in many areas, I remember being in that place when I **knew** my grandmother's cancer diagnosis; being in that place when my dad was diagnosed and knowing that the prognosis was 18 months diagnosis to death. But I knew when I needed to stay in what I called 'nurse mode' and not crossing the line into granddaughter or daughter mode. Then there was the worst time when I knew I was talking to my sister, my best friend in life, for the last time. And yet again, staying in 'nurse mode' because others (family) were depending on me to be strong, to guide and direct them through the medical world of 'what was happening' and what was next'. It was in these times when I felt like life was spinning out of control. When I felt completely out of control, completely empty with nothing to give to anyone. A time when I desperately needed to be filled. My cup was beyond empty, it was dry, I had nothing left to give to anyone.

I got through losing my grandmother. Struggled, really struggled losing my dad. He and I sang together in an acapella group, worship team and in choir. That was 'our thing'. So, when it was time to plan his life celebration service, my mom said I had to sing, which I did, for him. He was my hero. I was strong for him and for her. But that military twenty-one-gun salute, the finality of it all hit me and for a few minutes, this 'empty dry-cup' caregiver broke down. I couldn't help anyone because I couldn't help myself in those moments. Now I can say that in those few brief moments, there was a feeling of release of the burden that I put on me and I felt relief. But yes, you guessed it, went back into caregiver mode.

Then five years later my sister, gone, and I felt I had lost a part of myself. I did her eulogy because that's what she would have wanted, and I sang for her the very first song that I wrote. That day remembering our life together brought me joy and life amid her death. We did so much together, we laughed, cried, shared, danced, sang, and grew together. She was my confidant, and I was hers. She lived life to the full and I know that is something that we all need to do to the best of our ability.

I'm now still in transition. Now single/divorced and the grandmother of three beautiful girls and two boys. I'm at a place where things are ever changing, still. Still nursing and loving it. I've finally recorded the first song that I wrote and published two books. I have a home business, and I got my license to do real estate settlements. Still involved in church (not singing since the pandemic but help run our online service). Yet, things have changed for me in a great way. I have worked on me. I have found how I can use what I have been through to help others so they can avoid or try to avoid going through some of the same things that I did.

So now, I must take care of me, and I must advocate to and for other women (and yes for men, too) to take care of themselves! Advocate for this to happen sooner than later. We spend so much of our lives caring for others ... babysitting, caring for aging grandparents, parents, children, spouses, significant others, family members, friends, and the host of others that cross our paths. But who is caring for us?

I know many of you are reading this and nodding your heads in agreement with all that I have stated. I am sure that you have also asked the same question at some point ... Who is caring for us, for me? Or when will someone care for us, for me?

Well, that is where I was so many years ago, feeling stuck in that, PLACE! Where do I go? What do I do? Where does my help come from? If this was or is you, there is help and that help starts with ... wait for it ... **YOU**!

Not really what you were expecting? Well neither was I. But I hope that this, my story helps you to overcome, to get out of the rut and on the right path and that it will help you to help others get out, or never get in there in the first place.

As a nurse, I see so many in the caregiver, mentality and yes, I too was right there in the same cycle. Slowly, I was so busy caring for so many others that I started feeling the effects of the "doing too much"!

Have you ever felt rundown, overwhelmed, not sleeping well, irritable, poor eating habits, gaining weight, joints hurting, not feeling good about you, low self-esteem, low energy, just feeling like crud? Well, yep, that was me and that is where I was and didn't know where to turn, or how to turn it all around. But I knew something had to change, something had to happen because I was tired! I'm sure you can identify. We always go back to our mind game … I have so much to do, so many to care for. We are caregivers. I learned through an intense time of stillness, unplanned, that the caregiver must first care for self, to be the best at caring for others.

I knew that there were three elements that needed to be corrected so that we could be complete, be completely whole and able to care for others in the best way possible and still care for ourselves. You see that is the key. We are not caring for ourselves. So how do we do this when there is so much to do and so little time. We MUST make time for us so that we have time for those that we love and care for. So here are the things that we need to be complete. Our mind, body, and spirit. Here is what I knew. With a right spirit, it would be easier to get the others in line.

SPIRIT

So, being a Christian woman, I sought out the scripture. I had been searching for the answers and I knew that my help could only come from my creator, my God! I had heard different women in my church talk about going on prayer retreat weekends (something that I had never done). It all sounded great. They came back refreshed, energized. I loved the idea, but how could I do this with work, kids, husband, home, sick people, so much going on in my life? How could I get away for a weekend to spend it in prayer? Well, then I did hear discussed by some of the women to just take a day or even a few hours out of your day to be alone with God, to reflect, seek His face, His guidance, and His will for your life. It was all about taking the time to be still and to hear from Him.

Again, I thought of the 'How can I possibly'? Then, one morning I was off work (in nursing I was doing three, twelve-hour shifts). My Spouse had left for work the kids were in school and I was struck with the repeated thought of … do it now! Do what now? 'Come to me for a day of prayer!' Now that was God speaking to me! Remember, I was home, but that is not where this was to happen. Home had too many distractions, phone, laundry, cleaning, you know! So, in obedience and out of extreme curiosity to know what I was being called to do, I listened and followed. I packed a basket with water, bread, peanut butter, jelly, fruit, my Bible and left (I figured if it was going to be a day with Him, I better take lunch). I checked into a nearby hotel. Oh Yes, I did! Once in the room, I closed out the world. Curtains were closed, I turned OFF my cell phone, pulled out my Bible placed it next to me on the bed and began to pray.

Now this was not the most comfortable thing that I have ever done. The first hour was very uncomfortable, but then I opened my Bible and started reading scripture, just random scripture at first, that turned into guided scripture. This was so spontaneous and yet, so profound. I was in that room all day, praying, crying out, hearing from Him. It was exhaust-ing, exhilarating, enlightening, just an amazing experience to be totally, in His presence and at His feet. To be at one with Him, to be in His presences, to be still before Him for hours uninterrupted taking in all that He had, for me. All that He planned for me. He was refilling me. I was emptied by all that I had been doing, all that I had been caring for and He filled me, filled my cup.

Where does my help come from? It comes from Him, the one who first loved me, loved you. He is our help. He filled me in the five or so hours that I spent alone with Him. I was filled to overflowing. But He wasn't finished with me. He filled my spirit. I left that room spirit filled, knowing that this was something that I needed to do again to continue to revive my spirit.

But what about the everyday? I needed to be in His word daily, needed to be in prayer with Him consistently. Scripture tells us to pray without ceasing, that is what I needed to be doing. I needed to have 'time' with Him daily, not just when I was empty. If I stayed in His word and in communication with Him, I would never be empty, my cup would never run dry.

But I needed time for the important things in my life. So, up early, I'd start my day with Him. In devotion, reading His word, talking with Him, establishing a true and right relationship with Him. In doing that, I knew that with Him, there was nothing that He and I together could not get through. You see you get to a point where you talk to Him anytime, all the time, because you know that He's there and He hears you. He knows your heart, He knows your love for those you care so deeply for, and He always gives you what you need, just when you need it. He's an on-time God, yes, He is! So, you must make time for Him…your Spirit needs Him!

But what about the rest of me? My mind and my body? Well, that was coming, and I had no idea.

BODY

With a renewed spirit, I could see clearer as to other things that I needed to do, like eating better and losing weight. This would take time. Why? Because I was not alone in my home. I had a family, and they were not going to go for a big change in eating habits. So, I started making small changes. More vegetables, healthy meats, less fried foods, fresh fruits... nope everyone in the household was not feeling this 'change'. So, I got push back. I did as best I could.

But let's talk about eating right. In the world of fast food and crazy busy schedules and so much to do, how do you eat right, really eat right? Well, it had to become a decision. It happened for me over a long period of time. I tried so many things. Some of them worked, many didn't. I can say that some of the things that I attempted while the children were still at home did impact them, as they did pick up some of the good habits. So, know that what you are doing in the presences of your children, they see, they know, and it does make a difference.

They saw me as I started walking a few times a week. Then I started going to the gym and working out with my sister. I was finally starting to feel good about me. I 'felt' good. Weight going down, sleeping. I could handle the 'load' without feeling overwhelmed. However, things still were up and down. Life at its best!

I needed to get on track with my health and did with regular doctors' appointments, going every six months, not missing GYN check up's, making sure that I was taking care of my body, my temple. Remembering that we are only given one and we are to take care of it, we are to honor God with it.

I was getting the health thing totally under control. However, I continued to slip with the food, eating right, exercising… that is where I'm still in the struggle. But I know that even baby steps count as movement in the right direction. Look, I **do not** like to exercise, I just don't. I love to walk and that is something that I started back doing during the pandemic. I would do a good hour or more walk every morning. It was my time to work on my body and be at one with my God. Yes, I got up early to do it, but when you are filled with Him first thing in the morning and you've gotten a great walk on, now you can face the day and anything that it brings your way. Now my pitfall, winter. I don't do the cold, so that walking took a pause for the winter. Now I can't wait for spring so that I can get back to it. Yes, I really need to find some alternative for the winter months (or move to year-round warm weather … LOL).

I know that many of you are in different seasons of your life and wondering how to fit it in. Let me give suggestions as when I look back there were many times that I could have made time but didn't. As a young mom, put those babies in the stroller and go out for a walk. The fresh air will do everyone good. If your children are in activities, sports, parks and recreation, cheerleading, football, basketball, soccer, lacrosse, softball/baseball, whatever, while they are doing their sport thing you can be doing your thing, again, take that walk! There were always a group of moms sitting on the sideline waiting on the kids to finish and all talking about all that we must do and no time to do anything for ourselves. That was the PERFECT time for us to be walking around the field and encouraging one another to do better, be better for ourselves.

This also carries over to the high school years when we are the taxi service. Save that back-and-forth gas and just stay at the 'practice' and get your walk or workout on. I know, you say but what about meals? Here's where I somewhat tackled that one.

Meal planning/ meal prep even if you only do a couple days at a time. I see many are doing this and I wish it was something that I had stuck with. I do it more now for myself, especially if I know that I am facing a busy week. Prepare the meals on a less busy day or prepare enough for multiple days. This saves you cooking time once home from practices/events.

Going along with that is ordering groceries for delivery. I do this faithfully. I don't have time to go grocery shopping. I can utilize that time for other things. I order my groceries; they get delivered and it's a beautiful thing. If it takes you two hours for this process of grocery shopping and it only takes you 30 minutes to place your order, you have an hour and a half back in your day. Time for workout, time for God (filling your spirit & caring for your body). We can find time to work on us if we seek out the things that are available to us and use them as helpers.

So, I'm tracking for health and well-being. Knowing what I must do to keep my spirit filled, my body healthy… but the mind still isn't there. Still had work to do.

MIND

We must have peace of mind. Our minds must be clear. How do we do that. Well, it is as simple as taking a few minutes a day to be still and quiet without the 'noise' of the world, to clear out the bad stuff and take in what God has for you. Again, if it means that you are up earlier, trust me it will be worth it. Or, and maybe it means taking a few minutes from your midday (lunch break) and/or evening. Start with five minutes and then increase the time.

I started getting up thirty minutes early (it is now an hour) and for fifteen minutes I sat in stillness with God, just to hear from Him. Took that time to start my day with a clear mind, relaxing my mind of the worldly things, filling it with the things of God. His word, his will for my life. I started reading His word. I also read books that encouraged me, filled me. Books that reminded me that I am a child of a King, and I am here for a purpose.

We must be mindful of what we are putting into our minds. What are we listening to? What are we reading? What are we watching? All these things contribute to what and how our minds are handling our daily life circumstances. I stopped watching the news. It was depressing, *time* consuming and left me empty. I monitor what I watch on TV. Too much violence, negativity, degrading others; all these things are and can be impactful and we don't even realize it.

If you are the caregiver and you are not taking in positive things, you will not be giving out positive things to those you are caring for and you must know that this will directly affect how they are feeling/reacting/recovering from their circumstances. Being totally at peace with Him before I face the day; with Him going before me and with me, I could do and face anything this world had for me. I could care for others, because I had taken time to care for me, first. I hold fast to the scripture that speaks to this.

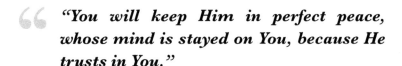 *"You will keep Him in perfect peace, whose mind is stayed on You, because He trusts in You."*

— *ISAIAH 26:3*

So, there they are, all three are on track, not always. Yes, I falter. I am human, we all are. I faltered in a big way after I lost my dad. I got so busy. At this time, I was a Nurse Administrator working fifty plus hours a week, singing on worship team, leading bible study, single, involved in community events, caring for my mom... just busy. I was in a life changing car accident one summer day that stilled me. For months all I could do was get myself up, showered, dressed, go to therapy and back home to bed. I could care for NO ONE! God used that time that I was still to speak to me. I heard from Him. He directed me, showed me His purpose for my life moving forward. Laid out exactly what I was to do. He set me on a new path to do His good work.

Things that I was not capable of doing. Or was I with Him leading me? He gave me His music, songs; He breathed His words in me to feed to His children through music, books, daily words of encouragement. It is because of that summer day when someone crossed a double yellow line t-boning my car and ceasing my busyness, and He used that tragedy to bring about His good work in and through me. I had to be stilled to hear Him because I was doing, going, being busy. He took that time to help me clear my mind, again; to fill my spirit with Himself and His words, His love. He used that time to heal my body from the injuries that I sustained. From there I was made whole and new in Him.

Your Call to Action: Let me help you be restored before you are broken to the point of tragedy as I was.

I know that the three work together, mind, body, and spirit so that we can be the best that we can be for the kingdom. To serve in whatever way we are called to serve. For many it is to care for others. But we must always remember selfcare is always first. IF we are not complete in the three, body, mind, and spirit, we can't and don't give our best to those whom we are called to care for, to love on, to be the feet of Jesus to.

He renewed my Mind, Body & Spirit and today I still work to keep the three completely in tack. I am now eating well, doing intermitted fasting which has worked well for me. Eating fresh fruits and vegetables, limited red meats and fried foods, low carbs, and drinking plenty of water. No caffeine no soda. I feel good! I sleep great and wake up rested, refreshed. I continue to keep up with my health appoint-ments with every six-month check-up's, yearly dental checks, and all the specialist that I have to see. I'm getting through the winter months so that I can get back to my walking and in the meantime, I do what I can (currently live on the 3rd floor and no elevator so many steps). I have a morning routine that keeps my mind cleared, my spirit filled. I'm in the word daily. I'm reading through the Bible in a year for at least the 7th time. I'm part of a personal development book club and have great accountability people in my life.

I know this may all sound like a lot, but it is all possible. **You** must decide and know that **you** are worth the time, **you** must be cared for so that **you** are then able to care for others. This is not to all be done at once. As I stated before, baby steps. Sometimes it may mean one thing at a time. You must pace yourself. Once you incorporate one thing give it time for it to become a habit before starting the next. There are more in-depth steps to this and if you desire more, I would love to help care for you in this process. We are separated but together in this journey. I would love to have you become a part of this program. I am working to reach out to help women/men in any season to move forward in this process so that they may become complete mind, body, and spirit. You can contact me via email at Karen@cupsoverflowing.com. You can find me at www.cupsoverflowing.com. Links are there for both Face-book and Instagram. I offer, personal, small group, and large event sessions as well as online sessions/events and I am available for retreats and in person events.

Regardless of where you are in your season or on this journey this can be done. It is never too late to show not only you, but your loved ones how important self-care is and how God can use us when we are complete (body, mind, and spirit), when we come to Him broken, He can use us. He meets us where we are and restores us. Remember I was completely broken, unable to care for anyone when He spoke to me and restored me, and He is now using me to do this very work! This work is my legacy to my family for self-care, and self-love. Before you can love on and care for those who need your help and guidance, you must first love and care for you. Our children, grandchildren, great grandchildren are watching. Be the good and right example that they too, may pass on to the generation's, completeness, love of God, love of self, love of God's children. Love, it is the Greatest Gift! Always remembering that you can't pour from an empty cup. Fill my cup Lord and make me whole!

Cups Overflowing,

Karen

ABOUT THE AUTHOR

KAREN CAREY

Karen Carey is a Registered Nurse, Business Owner, Singer, Songwriter, Author, and Internationally Recognized Certified and Accredited Coach (IAPC&M), helping women (and men) to become complete, body, mind & spirit. Focusing on filling cups to overflowing. Instilling self-care first so that one can give 100% to others. You can't pour from an empty cup!

Before starting a business, Karen worked 3 years in education, 10 years in the accounting arena, 26 years as a Registered Nurse (12.5 were management/administration), 10 years as a youth sponsor (volunteer) and 6+ years in women's ministry (volunteer). After a successful career helping countless others, and mentoring many, Karen now coaches on how to care for oneself body, mind, and spirit so that one is fully equipped to pour into others in a 'complete' positive and healthy way. Being filled, then filling others' cups in a positive way, that they too can then pour into others.

Karen enjoys singing, writing music, bowling, playing volleyball, spending time with family and walks on the beach.

Karen is available for your cup-filling session/private consultation, small group sessions, retreats, and speaking engagements.

You can reach Karen at:

Email - karen@cupsoverflowing.com
Website - www.cupsoverflowing.com

 facebook.com/Karen.cupsoverflowing
instagram.com/Karen.cupsoverflowing

FIREPROOF

KRISTINA INGVARSSON

I remember it as a feverish dream, but I was just exhausted from having been awake for more than 36 hours. 36 hours of brutal pain.

In that dream, I had made a decision. A promise to myself.

For the last two years, I had been listening to doctors, nurses, specialists, other healthcare practitioners and anyone who offered me advice.

Nothing had helped. I wasn't getting better. I was getting worse.

It was time for me to listen to the one person whose advice I'd been ignoring.

My own.

That promise changed everything for me.

I began to turn inward and to follow my own voice. To break free from everything that had been holding me back and to create the life I wanted.

That included a life without chronic pain. Something I was told by doctors wouldn't be possible.

I can't tell you how powerful it feels to step out of the victim mentality and take control of your own life. To decide, that THIS reality that I'm living right now, is not what my future will look like.

Especially when you've felt out of control your whole life.

I decided to follow my inner voice and what my body needed. It was a strategy that led me down the path of self-discovery like never before.

I went from being in survival mode both physically, mentally, emotionally and energetically. To recreate myself and move towards fully expressing my true self. I peeled off fake layers that I knew weren't me and I saw how it inspired people around me. In accepting parts of myself, I allowed others to feel accepted. Which in turn made me feel even more accepted. I became the kind of woman who leaned into herself and her emotions instead of trying to escape them.

I got there by doing what I was most afraid of; recognising and acknowledging all parts of myself. To eventually find my inner voice and allow it to guide me back to myself and who I was.

It's scary to speak up and to be heard when you've been quiet for so long. Up until that point, I had spent most of my life trying to fit in when I strongly felt I didn't.

Most days I was trying to figure out what was wrong with me. Why I couldn't seem to function the way everyone else did. I struggled so badly with expressing, managing and understanding emotions because I felt so much all the time! Something just had to be wrong with me.

For a while, I thought that if I could only be like everybody else, I would feel better too. This desire drove me to become somewhat of an overachiever. I was sure that if I got really good at life, I would succeed. I would be normal.

Yet, it was as if I was trying to be good enough, knowing I never would be.

I didn't know then that I had a superpower, as we empowered HSP (highly sensitive person) people like to call it.

I was highly sensitive and didn't know it. Not only was I struggling to process and express my own emotions. I was picking up and taking responsibility for emotions that weren't mine.

It was so overwhelming it eventually became too much and too painful to feel. I became so afraid of others' unmanaged emotions that I started to be afraid of my own.

A highly sensitive person (HSP) is someone who feels things very deeply. They are capable of taking in and processing more information through their senses than others. They are often very empathic and can easily put themselves in other people's shoes. One of the main struggles is feeling overwhelmed, which is a result of sensory overload from taking in everything that happens around them and processing it on such a deep level. It's said that 15-20% of the human population is highly sensitive. But it's a trait that is found in over 100 other species. You can learn more about HSP from Elaine Aron who has been researching this since 1991.

Like a vampire with their humanity switch, I found my switch for emotions and turned it off. It was as if I escaped my body to become numb.

I always describe this part of my life as walking next to myself. My body, as an empty shell with an invisible me right next to it.

I was desperately trying to return to my body to become whole again. But being in my body felt limiting. As if my flesh was a prison. Because in it I felt as if I couldn't be myself. That's why I needed to be numb and not feel anything.

Today I would refer to this feeling as though my physical body and energetic body were separated.

The thing about wanting to be liked and wanting to be the same as everyone else, is that it's in our DNA. Years ago when we were hunters and gatherers we needed to be liked. Because we needed to be part of a group to survive.

That's why when we want to go our own way, our whole being tells us it's dangerous. Stay the same, be like them, be part of your pack, or you'll die.

But that's not true anymore.

My body pushed me to a point where I had no choice but to stray from the group and go my own way.

This was what my intuition had been guiding me towards for years, but I had been too afraid. Too afraid to be myself in case I wouldn't be accepted and liked.

Truth was that in hiding I wasn't accepting or liking myself. But strangely expecting others to do so. And possibly show me that I was worth loving.

In becoming myself I thought I needed to rebel. To break up with everyone and everything. But change can happen slowly, quietly and gently. You can find the balance in it. You get to choose how and when you want to bloom.

 "When you share yourself with the world, be fearless. You only experience rejection when you first reject yourself."

— TJASA DORELAY

A close friend then and now used to describe me as someone who completely lacked empathy. Sometimes she even refers to our late teens as "before you started to care about people". She had no idea what was going on and neither did I.

Outwardly I seemed to be a somewhat confident, but shy girl, with a "don't care" kind of attitude. I listened to loud heavy metal music to block out everything I was feeling. And until a few years ago I truly believed that I wasn't an empathic person capable of loving and caring for others.

I had too much empathy. I cared too much about what others were thinking and feeling. I felt so much that I had to separate myself from it to survive. I know today that it's a common survival mechanism for HSPs.

There was a constant battle going on inside me. The girl who wanted to be like everybody else, people pleased like a champion and said yes to any opportunity to show how great she was. Being the best used to be my interpretation of what being successful meant.

Today I define success by how much I can be myself. Because it's in my expression of myself that I connect with people and create happiness and love.

I think part of me wanted to continue feeling like there was something wrong with me. Because then I wouldn't have to do anything about it. For some reason, we always seem to think that it's worse to do something than to stay in suffering. Even if that suffering is bad. That's how we end up staying in the wrong job or relationships for much longer than we want to.

 "Sometimes what you're most afraid of doing is the very thing that will set you free."

— ROBERT TEW

The action of pushing everything down to avoid feeling anything causes problems. When we bottle up our emotions eventually the jar gets full. It now takes effort to keep the lid shut, so some of those bottled up emotions don't escape it. A common result of this is anxiety.

I was 17 years old when I started to experience severe anxiety and panic attacks. Yet another thing I thought was wrong with me and that I needed to hide from people.

Nature became my escape. Out in the woods, I could panic in private. I would walk for hours and it helped me feel better and more grounded again. Nature is still my most important medicine.

More and more emotions escaped my jar because I no longer had the energy to keep the lid shut. I've learnt that emotions need to move through our bodies. They don't like to be stuck, which is why they cause us problems.

Trying to process these suppressed emotions was so over-whelming. I couldn't sort it all out inside my head. So I began to remove it from the inside of my mind and put it down in a notebook. This first notebook is almost completely filled with questions. And the most recurring question is: Who am I?

It was in my late teens that I started to become aware of my sensitivity. But I didn't know about HSP yet or how to deal with everything I felt. The increasing anxiety forced me to find new ways to deal with it. I switched from only writing in notebooks and started to paint everything I felt. My art journals became a safe form of expressing myself that no one would ever see or have the opportunity to judge.

Because I still desired to be liked so much, being judged felt like the opposite and became my biggest fear. I was constantly worried about doing or saying something that might upset or trigger something within others.

Right after high school, I moved back home for a short period. After having been somewhat independent in boarding school, this was difficult. I rebelled. I was done doing things the way society had decided was acceptable. I was done agreeing with people when I didn't. I was done not standing up for things I believed in. I was done being afraid.

But I'm an introvert. We rebel in silence.

Through art, clothes, writing and possibly in conversations with our best friend.

I wanted life to change so badly. To escape the show I was putting on to be accepted by others. Sometimes I would try to step out of my well-practised role to see how others reacted. Only to quickly draw back into my shell if someone as much as raised an eyebrow. I was tired of fake smiles and pretending everything was fine when it wasn't.

But I still had limiting beliefs holding me back.

Beliefs are incredibly powerful and often work on a subconscious level! I spent years with next to no self-esteem. I started to believe everything other people said to and about me. I was a master at interpreting every little negative hint as criticism and absolute truth.

Deep in my subconscious, was the belief that I was not worthy of love.

Rebelling against the world doesn't work when you have old beliefs keeping you from changing. And I didn't know the power of beliefs back then.

So I continued my silent fight, a fight that mostly took place inside me. Not feeling worthy drove me to have several jobs at the same time and work myself to exhaustion. I balanced on the edge of burnout for a long time.

All that time my body sent me signs that I wasn't well and I ignored all of them.

It wasn't strange that my body eventually found a way to force me to stop.

Our bodies are amazing. They are constantly communicating with us and telling us what needs our attention. But translating these bodily signals into what it means isn't always easy.

One morning I woke up with cramps in both my calves. After that my muscles refused to relax again and it was very painful. My body had had enough. I'm embarrassed to admit that it took me way too long before I went to the doctor despite barely being able to walk.

Sitting at the doctor's office I remember when she asked me about my mental health. I told her everything in my life was good at that time and it was. At least everything I was consciously aware of.

I also remember how badly I wished it was a mental problem. I used to think that if my mind had created this, then I can uncreate it.

Pain always serves a purpose. That's a scary thought when you feel so controlled and limited by the pain. But what is it telling you? What was my pain telling me?

That I couldn't keep pushing myself to exhaustion? That suppressed emotions can manifest as a physical illness? That instead of working so hard to please everyone else, I could work on myself to raise my self-worth?

Everything in health is connected. What happens in our physical body can affect our mental, emotional and energetic body if not treated. And the other way around. Even though I never found out exactly what caused my pain, I believe it was my deep emotional wounds that manifested as pain in my physical body.

Then the pain increased more and spread. It was no longer just my legs. It was my entire body. I started to feel hopeless. I was so scared that this was going to be my life from now on. To never again be able to do normal things.

My doctors went from trying to figure out what was wrong with me, to finding something that would decrease the pain. It was an experiment. We tested different drugs. Some increased the pain. Some were highly addictive. This one drug made me lose the ability to move the right side of my body.

At the time I was in my second year of becoming an accountant and I was stubborn. I wasn't going to let this stop me from my education. So when I could no longer hold a pen, I took notes on my computer. When I could no longer lift my right arm, I typed with my left hand. I made it work.

After 3 nights with no sleep, I wasn't a functioning human being anymore. I had no strength left. No more fighting spirit in me. I was exhausted. I had reached the limit of how much pain I could take.

And then pain saved my life.

Every time I'd been to the doctors they kept telling me that pain doesn't kill you. I hated hearing that. I kept thinking it could. That one day it would.

I was unfortunate to meet a bad doctor that day. When I told him that I could keep doing this, that I was too tired, he looked at me and said that I wasn't his problem. He didn't believe me. He thought I was faking it to get attention. He threw me out of the room.

I felt like I had lost my last hope. There was nothing and no one that could help me or even wanted to help me.

At that moment it felt like being pushed close to the edge of a cliff, by a wall of fire. Before things get really bad, hope allows you to see a potential future on the other side of the fire. But as you lose hope, the wall grows thicker. You start to understand what a huge amount of strength it will require to fight the fire. And since no one has taught you that you are fireproof, jumping off the cliff seems like the only option not to get burned.

If you're standing on the edge, know this: You are fireproof! The fire may seem scary and it may feel as if it will burn you, but the fire lives within you. You are part of it. It is part of you. So you can walk through it!

If you have done that, you already know how incredibly strong you are. Never doubt that strength.

I fell right outside the doctor's office. My legs wouldn't carry me further. I crawled to a bench, rested for a few minutes and called my brother to pick me up. Later that evening after a few hours of quite horrible thoughts, my dad drove me to the ER. This is where I met Victor. A man who couldn't cure me, but was one of the few doctors to show empathy. He asked me one very important question.

What do you need right now?

That question became my solution.

Half a pill of muscle relaxing knocked me out and 18 hours later I woke up with new hope, my question and a decision.

It was time for me to listen to myself. To put my trust in the only person I could hold accountable.

Most of us want to trust our intuition and we continue to wish for those intuitive nudges when we have been getting them all along. I had nothing left to lose, so I followed my intuition blindly.

"What do you need right now", is a great question to ask if you wish to connect with your intuition. But, you also have to follow it. That's how the connection grows stronger.

Every day I asked myself that question and I made decisions based on the answer. If I got no answer, I would choose to do something and then ask again: Was this what I need?

It was a two steps forward, one step back kind of journey.

A lot of my healing took place inside my art journals. It's also where I rediscovered the flow state. At first, it was only for a second, then a minute, then a few minutes, then hours.

When you're in a lot of pain, whether that pain is physical or otherwise, that pain consumes you. It's all you can think about. Because it's screaming so loudly within you. Being in the flow state shifted my focus away from the pain. It gave me a well-needed break.

If you look inside my art journals from that time, you find a lot of dark pages. Darkness was how I expressed anxiety, which I had a lot of. So I created what I call my anxiety paintings. I put my anxiety on a canvas. And if I tell you this next part, you have to promise to keep it to yourself.

My anxiety now hangs on my brother's walls and he does not know it. He just thought they were cool and needed some art for his house.

My anxiety didn't go away because I painted it. But it lost some of its power over me.

I illustrated how it felt, gave it a face, with eyes and named it something I thought was a ridiculous name. After that every time I would feel anxious, I would say: Hello Rune, how are you today? And its hold over me would be weakened.

Slowly, I began to heal my body. When you practise connecting with your intuition daily, it starts to speak to you. And soon you will know yourself and your body very well. I started to slowly express more and more of who I was. Always guided by my intuition.

Since then I have continued to follow my intuition and I've made a lot of decisions that other people have advised against. I've been called crazy and I own it. This quote by Ernest Hemingway is tattooed on my ribs for two reasons.

"Sometimes following your heart means losing your mind."

Firstly, people call you crazy when you follow your heart since it isn't always the most logical path. Secondly, because intuition is about feeling more than thinking and to get a clear answer we sometimes need to stay out of our over-thinking tendencies. We do this by being present in our bodies (feeling) instead of our minds (thinking).

After realising the healing qualities of painting I spent hours every day in my art journals. I also dove into alternative medicine because I wanted to know the cause of my suffering. That's how I was introduced to the world of healing, hypnosis, mediumships and Chinese medicine. I met some of the most amazing people through this. My old interest in herbal medicine and homoeopathic solutions grew again. I started dreaming of my own herbal garden since my one-room apartment was starting to feel way too small.

At 25 years old, I still had a few issues with my muscles, but most days were good. In May I bought a house in the woods, with a big garden just in time to plant a few herbs and vegetables. My new life was beginning. The new me was finally going to be expressed in more ways than just inside my journals. My house had space for a real art studio where I created art for myself, but also for my business as an artist that I had started 3 years earlier.

This is where I found my balance. Having a space of my own. Nature was close by. The freedom to express my creativity. The independence I was missing when I was sick and had to move back home. I felt a stillness and peacefulness within my body and I wanted it to grow. To consume me as the pain had done.

 "If you get tired, learn to rest, not quit."

— BANKSY

After such a long time of hopelessness, I could see opportunities again. I knew my body and my limitations, but I never accepted those limitations as permanent. I try to keep that in mind today as well. Whatever happens, it doesn't have to be permanent and my intuition will always guide me toward the best path.

It was in my mid twenties that I finally learnt about HSP and so many missing pieces fell into place. My deep emotions had been a big part of why I felt wrong and reading about HSP explained why. Most importantly it explained that it was normal. I was normal. I was not too sensitive, I was highly sensitive and there was a difference. Being highly sensitive came with gifts. But like a superhero without training, a gift can feel like a curse until you learn about it.

While recreating myself and my life it was impossible not to think about: what was the meaning of all of this? This happened to me, so it must mean that I'm supposed to do something with it. Otherwise, it was all pointless.

Art had played such a huge part in my healing that it had to be part of my future.

I found a course in therapeutic art and quickly became certified. I continued to study and be curious about the human body and emotions, for myself but also for this new idea that was starting to form. In 2019 I became a certified coach and started a new business. Today I am merging my 2 businesses, combining coaching with art. My favourite thing is to see the art my clients create and the realisations they have from those creations.

Intuition is a magical thing. It takes great courage to listen and follow, but you will be rewarded for it. If something feels off, it is off. Trust that feeling within your body. Trust it more than you trust external advice. Sometimes even when that advice comes from very knowledgeable people. Even experts. Because you are an expert as well. You are the expert on YOU.

Intuition however can be hard to follow if you are not yourself. To find your inner voice and to let it guide you, is to trust yourself. How can you do that if you are suppressing who you are, your needs and what you desire?

Becoming your true self will awaken your intuition and lead you to your magic. This is what you may share with the people around you and they will benefit greatly from it.

I've seen this in myself and people around me as well.

I reconnected with one of my old best friends a while ago. She quickly became one of my closest friends again.. I remember sitting behind her in the auditorium on the first day of school thinking she seemed so cool. I think she embodied some of the things I wanted to be; confident, expressive (she had a lot of green eyeshadow), and funny.

When we reconnected her light was dimmed. She had been told stuff. What was allowed and what wasn't. What was right according to people's standards and what wasn't. She felt trapped by other people's view of life, just like I had been. She held onto so much shame, fear and guilt. And it breaks my heart to see people hide their true selves, especially when they are pretty amazing human beings.

I like to think that my encouraging words and accepting energy inspired her to let some of that go and start trusting herself again. She did an amazing job and I laugh sometimes at the things she says today. Because it shows that she overcame it. She listened to her body and what she needed. That brings the most wonderful feeling of freedom; like taking off your bra after a long day at work. You can breathe deeply again.

I often think back to 23-year-old me. I remember what could happen again if I fall back into old habits and put myself last. I remind myself of this every time I go through difficult things. Feel the emotions. Feel them as much as you can right now. Allow yourself to be deeply immersed even in the shitty feelings. Welcome it, no matter how horrible it feels.

I tell myself: Kristina, if you don't feel it, the emotion will wander down into your legs and it will be hell all over again.

I express what needs to be expressed. It's not always perfect. Sometimes I forget. But then 23-year-old me pops back into my memory and I tune inward. I trust myself to be strong enough to get through it. Because I know I'm fireproof.

"Make today so awesome that yesterday gets jealous."

— UNKNOWN

And if you forget and stray from your path. Tomorrow is a new day, a new opportunity. Right now is a new opportunity. Thinking about how you failed only prevents you from doing better sooner. Forgive yourself and try again and again and again.

If you take away only one thing from my story, let it be this. You hold all the answers to your questions. What you are desperately searching for outside of yourself, can be found inside yourself. And only you can know if something is right for you.

There is more power in acknowledging your feelings than to suppress them. Learn to dance with your emotions and ride your emotional waves. You can even do so with pleasure. By accepting yourself, forgiving yourself and loving yourself. All of you. Everything about you. The key to doing that is also inside you.

You already know this, but life's too short to live according to other people's ideas of what success and happiness look like. Peel off the layers that aren't fully you. Find your path. The path your intuition is constantly guiding you towards. Explore your emotional world and express what needs to be expressed. With kindness in mind towards yourself, other people and the planet.

I promise that no matter where life has been taking you lately, you are strong enough. You are stronger than you think. You are more powerful than you think. You have more options than you think. You can change more than you think.

You are fireproof.

So let your internal fire burn.

Let it lead the way.

Home.

To yourself.

ABOUT THE AUTHOR

KRISTINA INGVARSSON

Kristina Ingvarsson is an Alignment Coach and Course Creator who helps creative and highly sensitive women understand and manage overwhelming emotions - to live a more balanced life intune with their emotional waves.

Before starting her own business, Kristina worked full time in accounting with art as a side business. After getting her coaching certification she merged her art business with her newly started coaching business. Apart from one on one clients she also teaches emotional management to companies and their employees.

Kristina loves to be close to nature, create art, drink tea and stand up paddle boarding.

She is available for private consultations and company workshops.

You can reach Kristina at:

Email: ingvarsson.kristina@gmail.com
Website: www.inspiredbykristina.com
Online shop: www.inspiredbykristina.com/shop

instagram.com/_inspiredbykristina_

THE WISDOM WITHIN

LEAH RODRIGUES

THE CRASH

I remember that morning, the morning that I didn't listen. It was on a warm summer day on a Saturday in July. I was driving along in my car, but I was not there at all. As was my life back then. I knew I needed to get there, I needed to see her, I couldn't miss it. I shouldn't have even left, was all I could think. I looked at the time and I recall thinking that if I could keep moving then maybe I could still make it. At that moment everything just felt like time was moving so fast around me, but I was in slow motion. I wasn't in my car at all, I was somewhere else. Where I should have been. I didn't see the car speeding towards me like a bat out of hell. It was too late. The car hit me and pushed my car along. I had lost control and may have even closed my eyes at this point.

My car stopped short of hitting a tree and time felt like it stopped still for a moment. In that present moment my mind could only think of being with her. I was annoyed and I was angry that this was going to stop me from getting there in time. I looked at my watch, if I was quick, I could still make it. The car had ploughed into my driver door, and I realised that I was shaking. My heart was racing. I was seven months pregnant, and I was out of control. My mind turned inwards and I prayed for my baby to be okay, "Please don't be hurt" I whispered aloud like someone could hear me. "I promise I will slow down, just let everything be okay" I said to myself. My internal voice resumed "I should have seen the speeding car, I should... ". I was just sat there staring at the tree that I had almost collided with, wanting to be with her. To be somewhere else.

When I reflect on that time, I realise I had reversed into another car only a short month before. Over ten years of driving and not one tap until now. At the time I wondered what was going on and why me. Looking back now, I wonder if the first time, had been a subtle sign telling me to stop and wake up; telling me to slow down. To be present. At the time however, I could not see it. I was not listening, looking or open enough to see it back then. The experience and events had been a direct reflection of my life. I was walking around with my eyes closed. I was smiling but inside I was broken. I was always moving, always pushing myself to do more, being what others needed me to be and refusing to slow down. No matter what I did, I just couldn't enjoy life and feel gratitude. The bottom line was always, I am not good enough! I wanted to escape the prison that I had created for myself when I was a child, but I just didn't know how. All I knew was that if I could just keep going and avoid my thoughts for long enough, just maybe I wouldn't crash. Well, the universe had other plans for me. That crash saved my life. It woke me up.

FORGIVENESS

I realise back then I was holding on to a lot of anger, holding on to so much pain and most of all to the blame and running from the shame. It was so easy to blame someone, to blame life for getting in the way of what I wanted. We often blame the circumstances of our childhood and where we came from. We blame our access to money based on our story and the beliefs that we made or were simply told when we were younger. These beliefs then prevent us from a different life, a better life. They will continue to prevent us from enjoying what we already have, always wanting more stuff, more love, more of anything to fill the hole inside.

I realised the only person that was hurting by the burning ball of energy inside was me. I realised I needed to be honest about how I felt and let go of my fears. For me forgiveness was one of the first steps on that journey. I started by writing a letter to forgive and thank those that had hurt me. I thanked them for the lessons and the strength that I found in me to survive. I decided to let go of the pain that I was carrying around and that I could no longer go on walking down the wrong road and in the ruins of my own self sabotage. The road that always led me back to the same painful place of self-destruction, self-abuse and addiction. I realised that forgiveness was accepting that what had been done could not be undone and that it could no longer hurt me. I would no longer hurt me.

> "A ship in harbour is safe — but that is not what ships are built for."
>
> — JOHN A. SHEDD

The journey goes on with every breath and every new day is a new chance to begin the life you want to see. I learned that my beliefs can be changed and replaced with a new one. I was told that I was a mistake, I was told that I was a failure, that I was thick and that no one wanted to hear my voice. I was told to shut up and keep quiet; to be a good girl. I was told if I could never stick to one thing I was never going to succeed. Work harder until you retire, do what others tell you to do. Does this sound like you too? Listen to the whispers within, they can be so subtle it may take some time to hear them. You need to pay attention. When something is meant to be and feels natural, it flows so easily, and you are success-ful. But, be aware of the imposter syndrome. The voice in your head that tells you that it must be luck or that it was a fluke because you achieved something in your life, and it wasn't hard enough. Well, I don't believe in luck anymore and I don't believe in coincidence' and neither should you. Only you make things happen for you and don't let anyone, not even yourself tell you otherwise. ***"Your thoughts become things and if you can change your thoughts, you will change your life"***.

As a child I wrote poetry and songs. I loved nothing more than to sing at the top of my lungs and dance like I was dancing for my life. I would not do it for anyone else but for me. After all I believed I should be seen and not heard. Particularly as I had been told once that I sounded like a strangled cat. I recall a story I wrote as a child was referred to as morbid and the look on their face told me all I needed to form my belief that it wasn't normal to write sad stories and it did not please them to see it. It was however my therapy, my outlet and a way of processing my world and how deeply I felt. All that was hidden under the mask would be released when I was in my room lost in a song. I recall my mum thinking I was going mad when I would wake up in the early hours to put a pen to paper. The words would spill out and came from the dark place within that I would ensure would never see the light of day. That no one else could ever see. Why would anyone ever want to read it, it was so sad. Nobody wanted to read a sad story.

On my 6th birthday I recall blowing out the candles and making a wish. While others were wishing for a toy or a doll, I only wished for future me to be happy. A vision in my mind as clear as a memory. I wanted to be loved, to love, to have family and to do something that I was successful in. To make my parents proud. In my mind I always wore a suit in that life. It is funny when I look back now how I thought wearing a suit would be a version of this success. Fundamentally, above everything I just wanted to be happy. As I grew older the target was always the same, for family, purpose and fulfilment. I would set a goal, then once I had achieved said goal,

I would feel the same knowing emptiness. So, I would set the next one. I would feel better if I got better grades in maths, if just lost a bit more weight, if I achieved a financial advisor status, if I had the top 10 most wanted items of the month in Look magazine. If I was just a bit more... I would be happy. The moment I achieved what I set out to do the next goal was set and then the next and the next. The bottom line was always the not 'enoughness' that I felt deep inside and the impossible standard that I believed I could never reach.

Have you ever felt so disconnected and moved around so fast like it felt like you had left parts of yourself behind? I never felt like I fitted in, not really. I had friends but no one knew the real me. I wore a mask to blend in and I don't think I even knew who I was underneath. I didn't like myself all that much and I felt so very alone even when surrounded by others I was lonely. It was exhausting. I would need to retreat to my place of solitude to recharge.

As I grew older my secret writing sessions became just that and I pushed the words away along with the big feelings that would go with them. I eventually stopped writing. I was told studying and getting good grades meant a good job. In contrast writing about feelings and stories to process said feelings wasn't a 'normal' thing to do. When I was asked what I wanted to be when I grew up, I would answer with something to make the grown-ups proud. Deep down I knew it was a lie but one that became imprinted in me like a part of who I was to become. I started to believe the words that I spoke. Along, with that script that I prepared I slowly became a version of myself that lived to please others. Although my answer to the question would change over the years, there was one thing I knew for sure. I needed to find my purpose and when I had found it, I would finally be happy. I knew that I wanted to make a difference, if I could help just one person to not feel so alone and small in this great big world, I would have done something right.

When I had my first meeting for this book, we were given a brief. Don't focus on the negative. The words stuck in my eyes like pins. Well, that is me screwed. I thought. When I tried to make a start on my story those beliefs that I had worked so hard to reframe came rushing back. But then I reminded myself that without night there is no day and without my experiences I would not be who I am today. They are part of my story and they have led me here to write my words for you.

I believe the universal power, your soul, your energy or whatever you want to call it whispers messages under the guise of dreams and synchronicities. We need to learn to listen, to spend more time in our creative mind and take actions towards the ideas that we come up with when we see them. So, write your ideas down, create a vision board, cut out magazines and go crazy because nothing is impossible. Everything and anything can be possible, if you just believe you can. Then you will.

A lot of people don't know their purpose. I used to think it was this one thing that I needed to figure out. I was torn between my multiple interests and passions and could not pin down the one route to take. When I left school, I had 6 jobs at the same time. I was a waitress, retail assistant, bakery operative, bar worker, paintball marshal and a travel agent. My cv read like it was written for multiple people. I later worked in corporate banking as a financial advisor, and I also worked for a charity concurrently – for 10 years. They were so different but felt perfectly in balance to keep me from boredom whilst also meeting my internal values. They also made me feel slightly broken and anxious like I was two very different people. When I was made redundant from both within a year of each other I felt so lost. I still hadn't found my one purpose.

After I was born, I lived with my grandparents for a while, then my nana unexpectedly passed one night holding me in her arms. This was just before my third birthday. I then moved back to Jersey with my parents. A year later an alcohol related incident forced us to leave the Island and back to Staffordshire. I grew up in a small council house, we didn't have a lot of money but there was always food on the table. I recall my mum would juggle the shopping money so that she could buy our clothes from the mail order catalogue where she could pay a few pounds per week. I used to dream as I flicked the pages of the catalogue each scene like a movie, I wondered if they had a good life and would daydream of a different life. I remember times when I would quickly retreat to the safety of my room to escape arguments so I wouldn't get the blame. Alcoholism, abuse and fear was a regular visitor in our home. Depression and sadness lingered in the air, and I never knew what the next day would bring. I would focus energy on what was within my control which was numbers, music and my body. Until my body no longer felt like my own. My wanting to fit in, to be loved, to escape and to blend in left me vulnerable to outside influences away from home and at thirteen years old I was raped. I wanted to die. It was a dark time and I spiralled compounded by my mixed feelings of failure and shame. A few years later I tried to share it with a boyfriend. I never saw him after that night. I decided to lock it back in the box and then didn't speak a word of it to anyone for over twenty years. I believed that it was my fault and if I didn't speak it then it never happened. I feared that if anyone found out then they would feel the same shame and leave me.

We didn't talk in our family. I knew that if I shared it with my parents that I would only sadden them. I didn't want them to look at me in that way. I was ashamed. My mother was so fragile that I didn't have the strength to help her through it too. After leaving high school I closed the door on the person that I was and created a new one, a new mask. I continued to focus on the things that I could control, the clothes that I wore and the money that I earned and spent. I thought I could fake it until I made it. If I could change my external image, then I could become someone else. I knew what I wanted and what I wanted I would go and get it. I would prove to my father that I could do something right. I created the life that I wanted but inside I was still hurting. I was not taking care of what was within or allowing myself to feel. I didn't believe that I deserved my life. I was an imposter in my own skin. A fraud. Don't let anyone see beneath the smile. Just keep smiling.

That younger version of me lived in the space between her two selves, her authentic self and the one who wore the mask, the projected self she based on what she thought she should be; what she believed others wanted her to be. what she believed the world expected from her. I looked for validation from my parents or anywhere where I could get it. I looked outward for things to fill the empty space. I would set goals and I busied myself with lists that I thought would bring me some semblance of happiness. Reaching those goals would only bring more of the same. That empty feeling would only remain within, and I would confabulate a new narrative of what would bring me happiness. The definition of a confabulation is story that you believe to be true. The voice of anxiety loves to do this and is a dear friend of mine, it confabulates a narrative that seems so very persuasive and then my thoughts give it power. It is a friend on my shoulder that tells me that I am not good enough, that when others are laughing, it is at me and that look they gave me meant something. What did I say? I must do more; I must do better; I must fit in. It followed me around and whispered to me. In my solitude it protected me from risk, from failure and from living. It held me back from action, paralysed by indecision, of not knowing who I really was. I had to change my paradigm. Everything that I believed to be true, everything I had been told, the boundaries, the limits on life and the beliefs that were ingrained into me. I had to unlearn it all.

Alicia keys shared once that she makes decisions based upon a feeling. If it's not a resounding yes than it's a no and it was liberating. I started to apply it and started to say yes to what felt right in the moment. If I am ever unsure, then it's a no. Simple. If something excites me, I will try it. If it doesn't work out, then I will continue to try what feels right for me.

 "You never fail until you stop trying."

— *ALBERT EINSTEIN*

The critical voice that is within is still there, however I have learned to recognise it and to also challenge it. I have learned to practically work through those feelings of insecurity and inadequacy that it would have me believe. I have a toolkit of meditations, mantras and journaling yes, but it still comes to visit now and then. I let the thoughts come and then I let them go. I accept the feeling that what is done is already done and what I can learn from it rather than what I should have done. There is no race or end line to meet. Sometimes we are in front and sometimes we are not, and that is ok. There is no number or scale to measure 'enoughness' and for so long I confused my own version of enough with perfection. The present is only momentary, and I try to spend more time in the here and now. That is the only truth. Everything else is a version of what happened and of what your thoughts will have you believe. *I am enough, we are enough, and YOU too are enough.*

I was trying so hard to create a person that projected a version of perfect that I had come to believe it was what I had to be. I carried the pain like rocks inside a body of armour that I had built to keep myself safe and locked away from further harm. In keeping things locked away to protect myself I was vibrating in a way that I was a closed book to all that was good. I wasn't true to any part of who I really was, and my doors were closed to anything that would bring joy to the child within me. I didn't feel like I deserved it. I no longer recognised myself and the pain only manifested in the parts of my life that I could control like food and alcohol. In embracing the darkness and accepting all parts of my story, I can now truly appreciate the sunshine.

Words for when you are at rock bottom from someone who has been there:

You have survived the worst to get here. I know it has been difficult, I know you are confused and scared living in the space between who you were and who you are meant to be.
That was me.
The you that lights up to makes others happy, and the home where your heart is free.

You endured difficult times, but you are safe here.
The journey you have walked makes you stronger, before you arrived in the place of fear.
Take your time here to just be.
To sit in the silence of that dark space that you have landed and to breathe.
You are alive, you are breathing, and you have a voice.
You always have a choice.

You can radically accept what has happened to you.
That it is not who you are and that above you are infinite possibilities, to be the person that you were born to be that those that love or have loved you always could see.

All of the stars in the sky shine uniquely and yet there is always room for more.
You are here and if you can find the strength to open your eyes, to move towards the only direction left that is up, you will find the door.
You will leave this place only when you are ready for more.

Let go of the rocks that you have carried for so long and leave them
where they fall.
The weight of your story is not meant be carried, but to serve as a
reminder from a time and a place
The pain of what has passed was to make space.
You can walk now.
The light shining on you is brightest from above,
what happened was part of the past to prepare you for what happens
next.
So that you can lead with love.

Place your hand over your heart, say I love you and listen.
If you are ready, you can now step into your next chapter.
The one waiting for you, the one full of adventure, joy and lives free.
Open yourself to let the light in, to rise above
from what once was to what is meant to be.

The answers are already there if you trust the voice within, listen, learn
and believe.
You were looking in the world for that which was already within.
Place your hand over your heart, surrender and rise
say I love you and let your life begin.
You are your own sunrise.

ACCEPTANCE

When I stepped out of the space in between, out of my own shadow, I felt freedom. Nothing that is worth it is ever going to feel comfortable. Just like a new pair of beautiful shoes once walked in, the pain makes your skin stronger, and they now fit you as beautifully as they look. It was not easy to step in, to something new and to embrace the unknown. I allowed myself to set down the weight, the goals, false expectations and the pursuit of what I believed to be happy. Happiness after all is a moment, it is fleeting and momentary. In a moment it can turn to sadness and emptiness. I thought I could fill my life with things, with goals and I looked for in others what I already had within me. I wanted to be loved, I now know that I have more than enough love for myself and to give to others. And so, have you.

I realised that in order to move forward I had to wholeheartedly accept the pain and the shame that I had hidden for so long and I had to choose to no longer allow it to hurt me. That I was no longer going to hurt myself. ***The past cannot be changed, it is only the beginning of a story that has no ending yet.***

Over the last few years, I have spent so much time lost in books, learning about philosophy and taking in the wisdom of those in the arena who are a step ahead. I practice daily gratitude and I look for the joy in every room. It can be as simple as the home that I have, the cuddles with my girls or a nice warm bath. Our brains are hardwired to store the negative emotions which goes back to our ancestors and their ability to survive. It can be a useful tool and those of us who are sensitive may have been the ones to plan and save a village once upon a time. But in these modern times it can feel like the thoughts are a relentless battle between fear and autopilot especially with world events and news. I haven't watched the news for a while now as it fills me with such a deep sadness that affects me to my very core. With daily anxieties you can also reframe your thoughts or let go of what does not positively serve you. For example, if we feel nervous about an exam or meeting it has the same physiological effect on our body as excitement does, the rush of adrenaline, the racing heart, and the bubbles in our tummy. We can learn to channel this it into excitement about that event. Imagine the best outcome and get excited. It takes practice but really works. I use it with my daughter, and it has helped her. By changing our thoughts, we can change our reactions, by changing our reactions we take better action. I live with a number of chronic conditions and as I see it, I can be someone with a condition who does not do, or someone with a condition who lives as full as she can. I am still working on finding the right balance but now I am listening and trusting. Our anxious minds can be useful when channelled in the right way but the anxiety of looking ahead, planning and safeguarding can also be detrimental to our wellbeing. The more we focus and look for the good the more we notice it. What can you be grateful for today?

I believe everyone has a story and I believe that our stories are meant for another. Stories have helped me on my journey. Listening to the powerful women who have overcome challenges and hearing about what came next was so inspiring. Listening to podcast interviews with Maya Angelou, Deepak Chopra, Lady Gaga opened my eyes to the lessons that we can choose to take away and how we choose to listen to our thoughts. That what happens to us is not who we are, and we get to choose what comes next. Those who experience pain can carry it like a weight anchoring them to a place in time, feeling the pain, blaming it and hiding behind the armour that we build only keeps us in that cold lonely tower. But if we look deeper for the lessons within the pain, we find our power, from loss we learn love & from our ability to over-come the worst we become the version of ourselves that we are today. We discover our strength. We are powerful because we are still here and believe me, if you allow it, the best is yet to come.

I recently came across a ted talk by Emily Wapnick titled 'why some of us don't have one true calling' and it was a lightbulb moment for me. What I once believed was a disadvantage or abnormal was not only acceptable, but it was my superpower! My ability to come up with ideas, my lifelong learning, and the way I would pivot and adapt to something new. There have been many names over the years to describe those of us with multiple careers and interests. A renaissance person, polymath, multi-potentiality and it was even once considered a desirable until our modern-day society tried to put us in specialist little boxes. I realised that the moment you figure out what the pattern of your joy is today, you are in your purpose. Look for creative ways to transform your passion into something that you can offer to the world. How this feels and the freedom it has given me has changed my world view. I realised. It's not to carry the rocks to the top of the mountain or even to the finish line, it doesn't have to be that hard. It is setting down the weight to climb or run weightless and to enjoy the views along the way – being present. Being present along the way, for me is enjoying the view of my life's journey.

If you have a passion or if you are like me and have multiple passions, try to take some small steps that feel aligned today. I started with taking small action steps when I felt inspired and before I could talk myself out of it. I even went ahead and set up a social profile where I share some of my words and another page for my love of interiors. I initially started with a pen name of course, but I acted out of inspiration and the sky did not collapse on me. It even has a little following now and I enjoy the community of it. What small action can you take today towards future you? I now enjoy spending time in my creative mind and also on my multiple passions, but I prioritise my goals and focus on no more than a couple at a time. With your beliefs and your words, you too can build the road in to your future. I want to help my girls along that road and if they want to jump or change direction they can and if they fall, I will show them that they can get back up and try again.

Our story has already begun, and you cannot go back to change what has happened, but you have the power to change what happens next. Every step you take is taking you exactly where you are supposed to be. You are strong because you overcame the pain. The sorrow has given you strength to take chances. Failure can be your friend if you look for the lessons that it gave to you, get back up and try again. I see you; I hear you and you need to know that you are loved, you are love. So, get out of your own way and live it!

I think back to the girl I was 10 years ago, a victim to so much stored up emotional pain that was kept locked in a box. The pain and the secrets had led her to a life of addictions to material things and beliefs that were unhelpful. She could not see a life well lived ahead as she was desperately trying to hold back what was within. Acceptance was the first step. Shame, doubt and blame no longer control take the front seat and fear will no longer hold me back from moving forward.

Today I am forty years old, I am a mother, a wife and I have a spirit that is boundless and open to the infinite possibilities that the universe has to offer. I have brought two beautiful girls into the world, two unique spirits that have lit up my corner of the world and now it is so much brighter. I have learned so much from them and continue to do so. Our home is filled with love and so much light.

As a girl when I thought about growing up, I just wanted to be happy. I would secretly wish on birthdays that I would grow up to have a family, to love, to be loved and to be at peace. I could picture it as clear as it is happening today. My wishes and dreams came true and so can yours.

What do I want to be when I grow up now?
A friend, a lover, a mother, grandmother,
who shares all her stories,
whilst living new ones.

The fact that you are here matters and the fact that I am matters. We are all here for a reason and it's what we do with being here that matters. We all have a story to tell, I am still writing mine and so are you too.

I am devoted to making a change and leaving a mark on this world. I hope to leave it a better place then I came into it. I don't know which way it will take me, but I will continue to follow the whispers and take inspired action. I want to live with infinite possibility and to show you that you can too. Keep learning, be open, give forgiveness and listen but most of all lead with love. Give it to yourself and give it to others. You can always make more. So, rewrite your story and be the most authentic version of yourself that you can be. You deserve the life you dream of. Take a step closer to that dream today.

A final message from me to you with love.

Hello you, beautiful you
I see you doing all you do
You work so hard and set your tasks
You do things for others, you never ask
Each day ends and you feel the same
Then go to sleep and start again
When did you listen to your heart?
The voice you had right from the start
When you were small you had a dream
The plans you made, the ones unseen
Those plans were whispers to guide your way,
If you listen again you will hear them say.
You are the one who holds the key
You design the life you want to see
To wake each day with a fulfilling glow
Just follow the crumbs and that voice will grow
You were searching so long, for something you knew.
You looked so hard, that you missed the view.
What you needed was already within
So, listen, give yourself permission & let your life begin.

Love Leah x

ABOUT THE AUTHOR

LEAH RODRIGUES

Leah is a heart led creator, wife and mother of two girls living in Staffordshire, UK. She lives with Ehlers Danlos Syndrome a rare complex syndrome that has caused lifelong conditions that affect her organs, joints & nervous system. A transformational and live well champion powered by lifelong learning and many, many passion projects.

With a background in financial & corporate services she has spent the last 9 years working in the social housing sector, supporting families with financial difficulties and facilitating IT development projects that enhance services delivered across the local community.

In her spare time, Leah has multiple passion projects qualifying as a yoga teacher, NLP practitioner & Mental first aider as well as completing a counselling certificate. During maternity leave she trained with the NHS and volunteered as a peer support worker to support other mums with their breastfeeding journey. Inspired by the fast healing shifts she experienced with Belief Coding® she decided to train and qualify as an accredited facilitator. She looks forward to helping many others with this amazing modality.

Leah is incredibly passionate about making an impact through the sharing of real stories to inspire and lift others as this has helped her to grow and cultivate her own pain in to purpose. With the freedom to embrace authenticity she believes that everyone has the potential to heal deep rooted beliefs that hold them back in order to design the life they dream of.

In between ballet and classes galore she enjoys spending time in nature, writing or listening to podcasts with a coffee in her hand.

For women who want to do it all and want to find some calm in the chaos you can connect with Leah here.

Link Tree: www.Linktr.ee/imLeah
Instagram: @ourhomeatthehawthorns
Facebook Page: @leahrodriguesonline

instagram.com/IamLeahRodrigues
facebook.com/Leahrodriguesofficial

WHAT HAPPENS WHEN A LAWYER MEETS NETWORK MARKETING...

LEANNE GABRIEL

*a*s a Johns Hopkins educated attorney, the last thing that I envisioned was to end up in the home-based business industry. If you had told me that my most challenging and rewarding journey would be in that profession, I would have told you that you were crazy! Why? We all have friends that have started a home-based business. We have been invited to attend a home party where the host is selling products and we are expected to buy something. Sometimes, we are even approached about joining the business. There are promises of extra income, financial advancement or even financial independence. However, we also know that in most cases that same friend will often stop pursuing the dream. They fizzle out and quit or maybe move on to try something else. Have you ever personally met someone who not only stayed in the game but went all of the way to the top of a company? I never had and I certainly never dreamed that I would be one of those people.

When I was introduced to the home-based business industry, I was working full-time as a discrimination attorney. I had no interest in the world of home-based businesses. I had bought some makeup from a friend selling cosmetics but I was just being polite and supportive. I did not even like the makeup I bought. My perception was that businesses from home required you to sell products and impose on your friends. I have never sold anything and frankly never had any interest in this type of business or in any type of sales. I was only passionate about one thing: empowering other women. That is why I chose to become a discrimination attorney. It was a career that gave me a platform to fight for equal opportunities for women.

But God had other plans for me. I went from being a lawyer and fighting for women's rights to being an entrepreneur and leading women to new possibilities. What a ride! I am so glad to share the journey with you.

The only reason I even entertained starting my home business was because of debt. My husband and I met at Johns Hopkins University. Johns Hopkins is a wonderful and prestigious but also **VERY** expensive university. When we got married, we pooled our finances and it was scary. We had massive debt, mostly due to student loans though there was a little credit card debt as well. We did the math and realized that we would be paying for a long time. With extreme discipline and a diligent plan, it would still take us over a decade to pay it all off. We were overwhelmed and did not know what to do. For that reason only, I listened when a client of mine asked if I would be interested in some additional income. I told him that I did not have much free time and I did not want to sell anything. He told me neither one of those stipulations would be a problem. His simple question started me on a life changing journey.

Let's start from the beginning…

It was Thanksgiving Day week and I was exhausted. I was counting down until Thursday when I could enjoy some peace and family time. When I became a lawyer, I decided to work at a small law firm because I was hoping to have work/life balance. I believed a smaller firm would lessen some of the pressure to put in billable hours and would allow more quality of life. I learned that smaller firms are more merciful but that it was impossible to avoid the demands of a legal career. On this Wednesday afternoon, I certainly did not anticipate that I would have to work on the holiday. I was finishing my work and then came the knock on the door. My boss informed me that the lawyers on the opposing side of the case filed a motion right before the courts closed for the holiday. They had intentionally timed this filing because they knew it would force us to work the next day and start generating research for our response. It was a tactic to wear us down. My boss informed me that I would NOT be having a holiday. Instead, I needed to be there bright and early the next day. After my boss left my office, I walked over to the desk of a more senior lawyer at the firm and asked if she would be working too. She responded with a yes and shook her head at me for even asking. She explained that we were representing the underdog and that large firms do this to small firms like ours. It was a nasty strategy having nothing to do with what was right or just. She sarcastically welcomed me to the real world of being a discrimination lawyer. She told me money and power would be used to try and wear down victims and their lawyers. That was a conversation that I will never forget. Sure enough the next day, I was in my office instead of with my family. Halfway through the day, I just shut my door and cried as I realized that this was my future. Nasty games between lawyers and no family life. That weekend, I talked to my husband in despair. I could not see living like this for another 30-40 years. I did not know what I was going to do but I had a feeling that I would not stay long-term practicing law. There had to be a better way.

As bad as this day was, it turned out to be a gift. What I now realize looking back, is that sometimes pain and disappointment are necessary in order to open our minds to other possibilities. I now understand that I needed to go through that experience. If my situation had not been this unpleasant, then I would have stayed the course. Financially, I needed the income and the security. I could not afford to leave and take a huge pay cut. In many ways, I felt trapped.

But when you are unhappy, you suddenly become open-minded. Therefore, when a client of mine asked me if I would be interested in another income stream, I was curious to know what options were out there. I needed to pay off our debt and relieve the financial pressure. He told me that there was a business that I could work from home that had no quotas or pressure. I could work when I wanted and determine my income. Then he explained that I would just help people save money on their bills. That sounded practical but it was certainly not inspiring or exciting, so I was initially hesitant. But then he told me it paid royalties every month when the customer paid their bill.... Well, who would not want to make royalties? That sounded great because if I could pay down our debt, I could have choices for my future.

In the past, some of my friends did home-based businesses where they sold makeup, skincare, jewelry, weight-loss supplements, etc, but I never wanted to participate. There is nothing wrong with those companies, but I was not a sales-person. In addition, I had no sisters to buy makeup and nobody in my family exercised. However, this company seemed different because I was not asking people to spend money on a product that they did not necessarily need. Instead, I was approaching people to save money, not spend money. These were services everyone was already paying for anyway. I decided to get started.

When I came home that night, I was ready to share my excitement with my husband. This was my first harsh reality. My husband did not share my vision. In fact, he believed it was a scam. He told me it was a pyramid, and nobody makes money doing these things. Then he proceeded to run a spreadsheet with numbers and show me how it would never work. It really took the wind out of my sails. I realized this would not be as easy as I expected.

But I shook it off and decided to make some phone calls and show him that it would work. Bright eyed and eager, I started calling people. I called some people to be a customer and others to see if they wanted to make money and join the team. My first call was to a very close friend that I had known since I was 15. I was shocked that she would not even listen, much less do it. Next, I called a family member who told me he would not join me or support me. I could not believe it. I started to feel like I had made a mistake and should not have started my business. Three more calls all produced equally terrible results. I was so discouraged that I wanted to quit. I called someone else who was in the business. He encouraged me and invited me to a training session on Saturday.

The training was very helpful because it told me what to say and more importantly what I should not say. They had specific instructions and even scripts to use. I thought it was kind of weird to use a script when I talked to my friends or family but the psychology behind it made sense. I realized that so far, I had been approaching it the wrong way and saying the wrong things. I was ready to go home, start fresh and use the right words. I was feeling positive again. There was only one thing that bothered me as I was leaving the event. I had seen speakers and trainers all morning ...but they were all men. Not one woman trained or was even featured as a testimonial. Granted, this was a service and technology-based company so I could see where it would attract more men than a skincare or jewelry company. But *no* women? I thought maybe it was a scheduling issue for this particular session.

Armed with new language, I made some calls and finally got some customers. I was still getting nowhere with building a team but at least I had customers to show for my efforts., I went from regret of starting to now having some hope of success. I called a friend and told her about the opportunity. She said it sounded great and would love to do it with me! Now I was excited! We planned to meet at a training near her on the following Saturday, It was about a 2 hour drive each way for me but I was so excited to get my first business partner that I eagerly told her I would meet her there. I confirmed on Friday, and she said we were on. The next morning, I put on my favorite dress and headed off to start my first teammate. I arrived early and waited at the door. I kept checking my watch as it got closer to start time. Finally, training was starting and there was no sign of her. After 30 agonizing minutes, I realized that she was not coming.

Why would she stand me up like that? I was back to questioning if I should be doing this business at all. I told my mentor what happened and he said "these things happen'. He told me that it is a numbers game so I should talk to some other people and move on. He also encouraged me to attend another training because I would learn what to say and also increase my confidence. I was drowning in self-doubt. I felt like I did not need training but instead needed different people to talk to. Discouraged but determined, I agreed to return to another training session. After all, Rome was not built in a day.

When I returned the following Saturday, I noticed again that all of the trainers were men. It really bothered me. Was this some kind of boy's club that I had stumbled into?

Finally at the end of training, I got up my nerve and approached one of the main featured speakers. I asked why there were no women trainers. He looked annoyed by my question and promptly told me in a condescending fashion that "none of them had earned it." He said that only the men had accomplished enough to be speakers. I did a double take in disbelief that he would say that and the tone he used when he said it! He clearly did not know I was a discrimination attorney. He was a complete chauvinist. Well, I was

NOT ok with his answer so I asked what him I needed to do to speak. He did not expect me to challenge him and looked at me dumbfounded. He said I must be a top producer for several months consecutively. Though I had no idea how, I was determined to do just that. I had to become successful enough that I could break the barrier for women and have the satisfaction of putting him in his place.

Looking back, I really need to thank that guy. Though he was rude and offensive, he sure did light a fire under me! Now, I had a goal and more importantly a mission. I committed to work twice as hard so I could be the first female speaker. I was more driven by my anger at him and need to represent women, than by my need to make money! This is an important lesson - we will often do more for a cause than we will for ourselves.

For the next few months, I spent my free time building the business. I still had a tough work schedule, but I would tackle my business on lunch hours and at night when I got home. I stopped watching tv and cut down my social time so I could squeeze in more time. Slowly, I started to see progress.

Then came my breakthrough! My mentor told me there was a huge convention everyone was attending. He promised that it would be valuable because all of the big success stories would be there and I could learn from the best in the company. I was very hesitant to go for two reasons: First, I had not even made enough money to recoup my startup cost. Second, my husband was still mad at me for spending the startup money and taking away from our social time. I knew he would not be supportive of me spending even more money and also traveling. But the more I resisted, the more my mentor insisted. When I complained about the time and money, he asked me how much time and money I had spent to become a lawyer? Then he told me one weekend was not a big ask in comparison. I was annoyed but I knew he was right. Feeling the pressure and filled with self-doubt, I agreed to go. Then he got crazy and told me to bring my husband with me so I could gain his support. That was an insane request.

I talked to my husband about going and of course he wanted nothing to do with it. But then in the heat of our conversation, he agreed to go but if the event did not sell him on the potential of the business, he wanted me to quit. That was terrifying. But off we went.

We arrived at the convention and I was blown away. There were thousands of people… thousands! Suddenly, I realized that I was not the only crazy person after all! Many of the attendees were new just like me but there were also experienced people who had great success. There were leaders who were full time in the business and had created amazing lifestyles for themselves. They didn't have to work for anyone else or have a day job. They just did this business full time and made their own schedule. Could you imagine? I was surrounded with possibilities. I was hooked! And even better, by a miracle, my husband was hooked too! I could not believe it. He told me that though it was not his thing, he would be supportive moving forward and wanted me to be successful.

I came home on fire. I had vision and I was a woman on a mission. Now I had seen it with my own eyes. I was walking differently, talking differently and speaking with passion and conviction. I started gaining more customers and people started joining my team. It was amazing! For the first time, I was tasting success. I kept it up for months and started receiving recognition from the company! That meant that I could go back to that pompous man who told me no woman had earned the right to speak/train. I could not wait.

I approached him and demanded (I did not ask) for the opportunity to speak and train. I was now a top producer which left him no choice. I was given a slot to do a small topic the following week.

I was ready. I bought a new outfit, put on some fierce stilettos and I was pumped. Right before the event started, I saw him in the hallway. He pulled me aside and put his hand on my shoulder (yuck). He said "You are the first woman that we have *let* speak and if you don't do a great job, then you will be the last." I could not believe it. I thought thanks for the pep talk. Good god. But I decided to use it as fuel and I went into the room determined to shatter his boys club.

It went great! And the best part is that when the event ended, other women came up to me. They were so excited to see a women speaker. I told them it was our job to outproduce the men and take our rightful spots. Within a few months, there were other women training. It only takes one woman to be the example. Nobody was going to hand us anything. We were making our mark. As for the guy that tried to block me from speaking, he ended up quitting!

Another convention was coming and I was excited. This time, I was going with a small team. Again, I was flooded by the energy, the freedom and the lifestyles. I saw people there with big teams. I admired and longed for their connection and camaraderie. This was nothing like law. They were having FUN! I didn't know you could have fun while making money!

Time continued and my results grew steadily. I paid off our student loans and my dreams were growing. There was a position called Regional Vice President and it paid unlimited residual income. I had my eye on that promotion. I watched other people achieve it and kept dreaming of it. I would set goals to hit the promotion but the dates would pass and I would fall short. As time passed and I did not succeed, self-doubt started taking over. I began to suffer from poor self-talk. I asked myself "why isn't this happening for me", "why is everyone else getting promoted" and "what is wrong with me". I kept working but I was coming to grips with the fact that I had plateaued and could not get past the mid-level position. I went to every training and talked to people but did not have a breakthrough or any big success stories in my team. It seemed that people were passing me. I felt like a parked car on the highway. The worst part was when people joined the company after me and then passed me. I realized that time is not your friend in this business. It will breed negativity and hopelessness. I needed to combat time and change my stinking thinking,

My mentor told me to start reading personal development books. He recommended authors like Jim Rohn, John Maxwell and Tony Robbins. Even though I had strong academic education and was an avid reader, I had never heard of, much less read any of these authors. But I needed a change and I was hungry so I dived in. Wow, there was a whole world of material that helped me sharpen my focus, defeat poor self-talk and most importantly start re-programming my brain to ask better questions. What can I learn from this? How can this setback back make me a better and stronger leader? How can I use this experience to help others in my team? Now these were questions that would produce great answers and new strengths. Questions and self-talk are the game changers in this industry.

I desperately wanted to be a success story and empower a team that was wildly successful. At the conventions, I studied the big leaders as they trained on stage but mostly I watched as they interacted with their teams. The camaraderie and energy was incredible as they gave out hugs and high-fives because their people were winning. I really wanted that but I kept coming back with my small, steady and average team. We were consistent, but there was no magic. I was going through an emotional struggle of feeling stuck, comparing myself to others and even imposter syndrome. These thoughts and feelings are what makes people quit the industry. I was determined to stay in the game. I really wanted to meet a woman that was doing well in the business. There was ONE. She was from another part of the country, but she attended the convention. I went seeking her and snuck down to the VIP seats to meet her. At that time, she was the only woman I could find that was having success. She was kind and encouraging. I hung on to her every word. Then I had a photo taken with her. I kept it on my desk and she was my inspiration. Maybe someday I could become like her....

Consistency pays off. I began to pick up momentum. I was having more success and more importantly so was my team.

We were in the president's club and the team was receiving awards and recognition. We were bonding and having fun like the teams that I used to watch. I was almost RVP.

As I closed in on the last part of my journey to RVP. I had to finish helping some people in my team that lived in New York City. Once they hit certain benchmarks, it would also push me up to RVP. I was so close that I could taste it. Then of all the crazy things in the world, 911 happened. It was the first terrorist act on US soil. It was horrible and frightening. My husband was from NYC originally and still had friends and family living there. It was devastating. It shook the core of our country and rattled us personally. And amid that fear, grief and angst, it also blew apart my business. Understandably, my NYC team lost all interest and focus at that time. It all came to a screeching halt.

Thank God for personal development because I needed it so badly at this time. I made a commitment to feed my brain for 30 minutes every morning, I took audios into the bathroom and played them while I showered, did my hair, makeup etc. That may sound funny, but it was a place where I was not distracted or interrupted. Starting my day with empowerment helped me to push through this difficult time. I sponsored some new team members to substitute for what I had lost in NYC and finally reached the position of RVP.

I was promoted at the next convention and it was amazing, When I came off of the stage, I was flooded with women from all over the country. They knew I was building solo and my husband did not do the business. They told me I was giving them hope. ME?! I was so moved.

There was only one mountain left to climb. It was to become a Senior Vice President. Very few people in the world had accomplished it. Our company was in over 20 countries at the time and so far only men or couples had hit that elite position There was not one woman who had built her business on just her solo efforts and become SVP. Here was an opportunity to do more than succeed, but to also empower other women to see what was possible as a woman building alone. There was a huge pay increase, but I was even more motivated to break that barrier for women. The question was whether it was possible to do that and be a mom. My son was young and I had a lot to juggle. There were no women to seek advice from….no example, no mentor, no role model. Did that mean it was impossible or did that mean that I had to step up and be that person…the first female role model. In fact, if I did not do it, who would? If I did it, could I open the door for other women?

Thus began the craziest journey. Constantly doing presentations, coaching and training . There was no zoom or video technology at the time so I was flying around the country. I felt so guilty when I left home to do meetings. My son did not want me to go and I felt like a bad mother. But then my husband told me to stop feeling guilty. He said our son was only upset for about 5 minutes after I left and then he went back to cartoons and was fine. Our son was my pride and joy and my husband reminded me that our son felt very loved. Also, what I was building would change our son's life when it was done. This was a willable and inheritable income. I realized that my travel was a short-term sacrifice.

This brought me back to the power of questions. Instead of asking whether I was being a bad mother, I needed to ask how this could make me a great mom. Questions change everything! It occurred to me that there was an opportunity to include my son and make this a valuable experience. I could use it to teach life lessons about goal setting, hard work, delayed gratification and getting back up after disappointments and setbacks. These lessons are not taught in school though they are critical to success in life. This was a real-life chance to help him. I explained the goal to our son and what steps had to happen. We sat with magic markers and made a chart. Each day, we would mark the chart. Somedays were good and some days were a flop, but I explained to him that was part of any great challenge in life. Then I told him that if he learned from this journey and talked with me each day, he would get his first pet when it was over. This was a lesson in delayed gratification.

Becoming a Senior Vice President required me to promote other RVPs within my organization.

Not only did I become the 1st solo female SVP, but the required RVP promotions in my team were all achieved by women! We had the first mother-daughter team, the first female team to become RVP in under a year, the first female partnership, the first lawyer, etc. We proved women can do it all!

This long and bumpy journey changed who I am as a person and more importantly changed my family life. My husband also quit his job and become a self-employed entrepreneur working from home. He became my biggest supporter and has been my rock. We have freedom to make our son our priority. We go to every game, every parent-teacher meeting and are waiting for him every day when he gets home from school. He is a straight A student, an athlete and is in an environment filled with love. It was all worth it.

The home-based business industry paints a picture of glory, recognition and freedom. All of that is true and obtainable. But what the industry does not share is what it will take to get there. It is a journey like no other. It will force you to face fear, rejection and criticism. You must learn to master your emotions and your self-talk. But if you commit to pushing through, not only can you have it all, but it will develop and change you in ways that you cannot even imagine.

My journey was tough and sometimes lonely, but I would not change a thing. Each struggle, heartbreak, disappointment and even the discouraging words were bricks in the foundation of our current life.

I have now been an SVP for over a decade. I have travelled the world speaking in front of crowds of up to 20,000 people. This journey has blessed me with some of my closest and most valued friendships. My goal remains to continue to pour into women and try to empower them not only financially, but also to lead them into the world of personal development. I mentor people to have success in the business. I also founded a free Facebook women's group and YouTube channel call "SLAE with Leanne Gabriel". SLAE means She Leads And Empowers. We feature women speakers each week that are making a difference by running non-profits, writing books, breaking barriers etc. What I have learned is that a woman alone has power but together we have unstoppable impact.

As you finish this, I would hope to inspire and challenge you to think big and long-term. Whether you are building a business, working at a company, or leading in your community, it is important to realize that what you do will impact many others. Pushing through difficult times and forcing yourself to grow will not only create your best version of you, but it will impact countless other people. Your friends, family and co-workers will watch you, feed off of your courage, and take bigger steps themselves. Those steps will then influence the people in their lives. You can choose to be the pebble that hits the pond and starts the ripple effect. Or you can choose to be even bolder and be a large rock that splashes that pond. Either way, just hit the water, make a difference, and live your best life.

ABOUT THE AUTHOR

LEANNE GABRIEL

Leanne Gabriel is an entrepreneur, global speaker and mentor in the home-based business industry.

Before becoming an entrepreneur, Leanne worked as a discrimination attorney. She obtained her undergraduate degree from Johns Hopkins University and then her JD from University of Baltimore School of Law. After a successful career fighting corporate discrimination, Leanne now helps people succeed in an equal opportunity environment with unlimited income potential. She is also the founder of a women's empowerment group called SLAE with Leanne Gabriel.

Leanne is a fitness addict and dancer who loves music. She is grateful for her amazing marriage and their son who is their pride and joy.

Leanne is available for speaking engagements as well as private coaching sessions.

You can reach Leanne at:

Email: leanne@leannegabriel.com.
Website: www.leannegabriel.com

Leanne's Women's Empowerment group is SLAE - She Leads And Empowers with Leanne Gabriel:

Website: www.SLAEwithLG.com
Facebook: https://www.facebook.com/groups/sheleadslg
YouTube – SLAE with Leanne Gabriel
Instagram: SLAE_with Leanne

facebook.com/leannegabriel.esq

instagram.com/leannesvp

THE ANSWER WAS INSIDE HER ALL ALONG

LORRAINE DAVIES

DEDICATION

*D*edicated to the most important people in my life who have made me who I am today

In loving memory of my Dad, Nick Davies 1959-2020 and my mother, Vanessa Davies

To my gorgeous children, Felicity, Sebastian and Ariya.

I am proud of you simply for being you. Always follow your heart in all that you do.

To my partner Adam.

Thank you for your unwavering love and support and for believing in me even when I didn't believe in myself.

And to you, the reader.

May you be courageous and choose a life of purpose, abundance and joy.

~

I had no idea where to begin, but I was going to change my life.

Riddled with anxiety and in the depths of depression, on the outside, it was impossible to understand why I was falling apart. I had everything going for me; a great job and a loving family, yet inside I couldn't get away from the truth of how I felt. I felt empty and I felt not good enough. Despite this, I knew that I was made for so much more and I knew I could not and would not settle for a mediocre life.

Fast forward 11 years and I will be forever grateful to the woman I used to be for her courage. It is never easy to admit that your thoughts, beliefs, and habits are at the root of your pain. But once you are courageous enough to admit this, then the journey to who you truly are can begin.

Courage has been a huge factor throughout so much of my life story. It was courage that enabled me to leave a job that was causing me stress and anxiety and begin my path as an entrepreneur. It was courage that empowered me to have the painful and heartbreaking conversation with my husband that initiated our separation and subsequent divorce. It was courage that enabled me to be at my Dad's bedside as he drew his last breaths. It was courage that inspired me to launch my coaching business and to coauthor this book.

But most of all it took courage to look within and it took huge courage to begin.

For so long I had no idea the impact the beliefs I had about myself, others and the world were having on the way I lived my life.

I couldn't understand why there was never enough time or energy left for me and why I felt resentful, anxious and overwhelmed. I couldn't understand why I would repeat cycles of procrastination and self-sabotage every time I set goals. I couldn't understand why whatever I did just never felt like 'enough' and why happiness seemed so elusive.

But what I did know was that the more I 'failed' the louder my inner critic became. I was constantly overthinking and over analysing and I was forever in comparison mode. I was constantly plagued by self-doubt, anxiety, and a crippling fear of what others thought of me.

In a bid to be liked by everyone I became the ultimate people pleaser; hardworking, over-giving, and putting my needs last, I frequently felt burned out and out of balance. My perfectionist streak held me to unachievable high standards. I constantly strived to be, do and have more in the hope that it would bring me the evidence I needed – that I was good enough.

But I was wrong.

As I look back on my life there were so many signs that I was heading down the wrong path. The intuitive nudges and physical symptoms in my body that I chose to ignore. The more I sought acceptance, praise, and validation from others, the further I moved away from who I truly was and the happiness and success I desired.

If you recognise yourself in my story, I urge you to give yourself permission to STOP, breathe, and practice self-compassion. You are doing the best you can with what you know right now, but you are not the sum of your belief systems. Your thoughts do not have to limit or define you or what you achieve in your life. You do not have to keep replaying the same patterns of procrastination and self-sabotage. You get to choose.

You get to choose to be courageous, to take responsibility for where you are right now, and to change it. You get to choose to let go of everything that is holding you back. You get to choose to trust yourself and follow your intuition. You get to choose to get to know who you truly are, to understand what lights you up, and to take action towards these things despite fear. You get to choose to accept that sometimes you will get it wrong and, in those moments, you get to choose to forgive yourself.

Growing up I was fortunate to come from a home where I was raised by loving parents. As one of three girls, I now recognise the privilege of my upbringing. We had a beautiful home; we took part in hobbies that we loved and were rarely denied any opportunities that came our way.

My mum stayed at home to raise us. Our house was clean, we had dinner on the table every night. She supported us throughout school and was the secretary of the Parent-Teacher Association. She spent a large portion of her time being our taxi service taking us to dance classes and music lessons etc. She was a Rainbow, Brownie and Guide Leader and our GirlGuiding UK District commissioner. My mum was always busy doing everything for everyone else. She had a hard time saying 'no' and didn't like letting others down. As a result, her needs usually came last. As my number one role model, it is little surprise that as I grew up, I have often expected the same of myself.

My father (the main breadwinner) worked hard all of his life providing for my mum and his three girls. As an engineer and later as a service manager, it wasn't unusual for him to work late into the evenings and at weekends. He was meticulous and always did his best and he expected nothing less from those around him. Growing up I felt a responsibility to live up to these expectations which led me to excel academically and always drove me to look for opportunities to push myself to achieve more. It is easy to see where this exceptional work ethic came from.

I grew up believing that I had to work hard and always do my best and I grew up believing that being a good person and a good mum meant putting other people's needs before my own. These beliefs however were not the root of the problem.

Showing up in the form of perfectionism, procrastination, self-sabotage, people-pleasing, and social anxiety I had a core belief that I was not good enough.

I remember hearing the phrase "It's not good enough" when I was growing up, but not once did my parents tell me that I wasn't good enough. They didn't need to. Viewing the world through the lens of my belief systems the feeling that I was not good enough haunted me well into my adult life and was accompanied by a web of other beliefs. These included; I had to work hard to be good enough, If I was perfect then I was good enough and I had to be perfect for others to like me.

To 'be perfect' I developed a ridiculous work ethic, constantly pushing myself to do more and be better. My focus was on how I could prove that I was good enough, working hard, pushing and hustling, striving and struggling. I believed that the harder I worked the more successful I would be and the better I would feel about myself. Life felt stressful and it felt difficult.

I found it hard to recognise, let alone celebrate my successes, never felt proud of myself for anything and I found it impossible to accept compliments from others always believing them to be ingenuine. How could somebody possibly think that something I had done was good or even great when I didn't believe it myself. Every time I achieved something I would simply focus on the next step, the next goal. Forever moving the goalposts meant that achieving 'good enough' was ever elusive.

Overcritical and over-analysing everything, I always looked for evidence that I should have done something better. When I made mistakes, which inevitably I did, or when someone offered feedback on my efforts, I could only see the negative. I could only see my flaws.

For so long I tried to be better, I tried to do more, I tried to be good enough.

In 2011 I experienced the first of several mental health challenges. At the time I was a lecturer teaching Musical Theatre at a Further Education College (for the record teaching and perfectionism DO NOT go together!) With a never-ending workload and in my bid to do things perfectly my work hours became longer and longer. It wasn't uncommon for me to be awake in the early hours of the morning marking assignments or preparing lessons. Before long I was clearing my diary of all the things I loved and that bought me joy to spend more time working.

The more I worked the more overwhelmed I felt. It didn't seem to matter what I achieved; it was never enough. I was so out of alignment with who I truly was that I developed anxiety and depression as a consequence. However, the notorious people-pleaser inside of me refused to admit that I was struggling. She refused to admit that I needed help. I hated disappointing others or feeling that I had let them down so I pushed and struggled and I worked harder until I broke.

I'm not sure that those around me knew how to support me at this time and it's no wonder - I shut out the world and retreated to my sofa. Sitting in my nightie with the curtains closed, unable to function, I felt empty and I felt not good enough.

In the summer of 2011, I was introduced to Cognitive Behavioural Therapy which forced me to begin to unpick my thought patterns and explore the impact they were having on my life. Frankly, I was horrified at some of the thoughts I was having every day and how I spoke to myself when no one else was listening. Yet I was fascinated by the idea that I had the power to change the beliefs and habits that had been so ingrained since childhood.

By March 2012 I had decided to leave the teaching profession. As is the way with the universe, as one door closed, another opened - I was introduced to a business opportunity by a friend. I was attracted to the confident and self-assured leaders that I met and intrigued by a business that promised personal growth alongside an income.

I spent the next few years growing myself and my business. Every time my business hit a plateau I could see the correlation – it was my thoughts and beliefs that were holding me back, not my skills. As I put more time and energy into growing myself my business grew too. I got good at focusing on the positive in life and was excited and optimistic for my future. I became more courageous and more confident and I grew in self-belief. In 2016 I hit a milestone in my business and was promoted to the top 3% of my company.

On the outside, everything looked perfect. But whilst my business was thriving my belief that I was not good enough was playing out in other ways. Poor investments and over-spending over the past 4 years had caught up with me and I was in crippling debt. I was using credit cards to pay the interest on other credit cards. The more money I borrowed, the worse the debt became.

In April 2017 I received my biggest commissions cheque ever, ironically it was also the month that I cut up all my credit cards, called all my creditors, and told them I couldn't pay. I was so ashamed. I didn't understand how someone I considered to be intelligent could have got themself into such a horrendous situation.

Later the same year my marriage broke down. If I am honest with you and with myself, the personal growth journey that I had been on over the past 5 years had changed me. I wanted more from my life. I had big dreams and goals and a vision for where I was going and the lives I wanted to change. As I grew, we grew apart. It took an enormous amount of courage to face this truth. But for the first time in a very long time, I trusted my intuition and initiated the conversation with my husband that led to our separation and divorce. Even though my heart knew that it was the right thing to do, it was one of the hardest decisions I have ever made.

The breakdown of my marriage triggered something inside of me. Once again it highlighted my feelings of unworthiness and of not being good enough. I was full of guilt about the consequences my actions may have on my children. I was filled with shame about my debt and I felt like every decision I made was letting other people down. I began to put a huge amount of pressure on myself. I needed to grow my income to provide for my children and to pay back my debt. I easily slipped back into my default habits of overworking, pushing, striving, and struggling. No matter how hard I worked my business and my income continued to nose dive. I felt forced to return to teaching in a bid to create more financial security in my life.

In November 2019 I received the news that no child wants to hear, that my Dad had been given a diagnosis of terminal cancer. I think I dealt with it as many other people would, first I felt disbelief, (surely it must be a bad dream), followed by heartache and absolute sorrow. In the run-up to my Dad's diagnosis I was caught up trying to be superwoman - working part-time as a supply teacher, running my business, looking after 2 small children, trying to be a good partner, running a house and I was also 7 months pregnant. I thought I had to do it all, I thought I had to be everything to everyone (sound familiar?).

You would think that after the initial shock of my Dad's diagnosis that I would have taken this as a sign to slow down and enjoy life, but that simply wasn't the case. I increased my workload in my business, working into the early hours of the morning speaking to women across the other side of the world. The month before my Dad passed away I had the most successful month in my business for 3 years, despite having a 4-month-old baby and homeschooling a 5 & 6-year-old all amid a pandemic. But at what cost? As I look back, I am sure that my 'just keep going' mantra gave me something to focus on other than my Dad's diagnosis, but it was yet another example of me repeating old patterns.

On the 9th of June 2020, my Dad passed away surrounded by his girls. It was one of the most challenging and humbling experiences. When someone close to you dies you notice the fragility of life. It would have been easy to fall into the victim mentality of life not being fair, but instead, my Dad's death gave me perspective. It served as a wake-up call. My beliefs and habits of the past 33 years weren't making me happy or moving me closer to the life I wanted to create. I could choose to stay where I was or I could choose to change.

Things didn't happen overnight. It's one thing knowing and acknowledging that something has to change, but it's something different altogether committing to do the healing work that is so often required.

In April 2021 the universe gave me a huge nudge. Struggling with fatigue, dizziness, nausea, low blood pressure, and a string of other health challenges I was frustrated by a lack of physical diagnosis. The reality was that the unprecedented stress of the previous 4 years was finally taking its toll on my body. In an attempt to reclaim my life, I began working with a nutritionist to rebalance my hormones and gut health. Alongside improving my nutritional intake, she also suggested that I began practices for reducing stress introducing me to yin yoga and reminding me of the power of mindfulness and meditation. My healing process was not a quick fix but as each day and week passed, I began to reclaim my life. As I did, I decided that I was no longer going to attempt to plaster over the cracks in my foundations with affirmations and positive thinking, but instead, I was committed to a journey of self-discovery, healing and growth.

I began to reflect on the things in my life that were feeling amazing and joyful and the things that no longer felt that way. I recognised that I was lacking a sense of fulfilment and joy in my career. The more I thought about it I realised that I had been holding myself back from doing anything different because I was scared. I was scared of letting others down, I was scared about what others would think of me, and I was terrified of failing again.

So, I did something radical. I decided to let go of these thoughts and feelings and take action despite all the fear. At that moment I set some exciting, yet terrifying goals for myself – I would become an accredited life coach and I would write a book (well a chapter will do for now!).

As I let go of the things that I had been clinging to so desperately out of fear, I made space in my life for miracles to occur. I stumbled across a coaching certification that aligned beautifully with who I am and as I began to work on becoming a coach so that I could help others transform their lives, I went through a transformation of my own.

I got to truly know myself. I got really clear on my values and what is important to me and I began to focus on living on purpose, doing things that bring me joy. I learned to identify when I felt great and when things felt 'off' and what I could do about it. I became aware of my thoughts and what I said to myself when no one else was listening. I began to notice what triggered me and the patterns in my thoughts and behaviour. I committed to learning to trust, in myself, in others, and the universe. I began to listen to my intuition and make decisions based on this, not allowing other people's opinions to throw me off course. I learned to accept that I was exactly where I was meant to be in life and I decided to reframe past experiences in a more loving and accepting way. I began forgiving others that I felt had wronged me, but more importantly, I began to forgive myself.

Every step of my transformation led me to this; the understanding that we all have an inner guidance system within us that knows the next best step. It knows your values, your priorities, and your passions and it is always available to guide you towards a life of purpose, abundance, and joy. But so many of us have forgotten how to listen to our intuition and how to use it to navigate our lives. Instead, we fall into the habit of looking outside of ourselves for proof that we are on the right path, that we're doing the right thing, and that ultimately, we are good enough.

But the answer was never outside of you.

When you insist on looking outside of yourself for guidance and for validation you run the risk of living life as per others' expectations, living in the 'should's', the 'must's' and the 'have to's', falling victim to your perceived obligations and responsibilities. You find yourself adopting beliefs about yourself, others, and the world that were not even yours, to begin with.

When you focus on living up to others' expectations of you, you will never feel whole, you will never feel complete, and you will never feel good enough. You will continually find yourself caught up in patterns similar to mine; perfectionism, procrastination, people-pleasing, and self-sabotage. You will lack self-belief and self-trust because you are failing to do the one thing that matters the most. To get to know who you truly are, understand what matters to you, and live your life according to this. If you do not take the time to listen to yourself and what it is that YOU truly want, your life will always feel like something is missing.

The beautiful thing is that you ALWAYS have a choice. It doesn't matter how long you have been ignoring your intu-itive nudges or allowing yourself to feel unseen, unheard, and unvalued, all it takes is the courage to begin.

When you decide to prioritise yourself, every single day and give yourself permission to stop, breathe, and tune in you will begin to feel 'seen' and 'heard' and valued because YOU, see, hear and value yourself.

You have the opportunity right now to choose you.

Through quiet meditative practice/journaling you get to raise your awareness of what you have been doing up until this point in your life. Everything starts with awareness.

Do you know what you say to yourself when no one is listening? Are you kind and compassionate or are you critical and judgemental? Do you recognise patterns in your thoughts? For example, thoughts that come up multiple times a day. Are you aware of habits that might be keeping you stuck, such as self-doubt, self-sabotage, or people-pleasing? Do you know what triggers these habits?

All of this awareness can help you to identify which thoughts, beliefs, and habits are no longer serving you; those that are stopping you from living a life of unlimited purpose, abundance, and joy. You can then choose to let them go.

This process doesn't have to be hard; it doesn't have to be complicated and it doesn't take carving out hours every single day, but it does require a commitment to work through thoughts and feelings that are not always comfortable and it does require practice. On the plus side, the more you practice, the easier it all becomes and the rewards will honestly be life-changing.

You will have absolute clarity on who you are, your values, passions, and priorities. You will recognise that you can check in with your emotions to identify whether you are heading down the right path (feeling joyful) or deviating away from who you truly are (feeling anxiety, sadness, anger, fear). You will be able to understand if you are making decisions from a place of love and joy (your intuition, your higher self) or scarcity and fear (Ego). With all of this knowledge about yourself, you have the opportunity to create radical change.

You have the opportunity to make decisions for your life based on your intuition, decisions that come from a place of alignment and integrity and that feel exciting, joyful, and expansive. You get to trust yourself and to trust your decisions. The more you do this, the easier it will be to quiet the noise of others' expectations and to let go of the fear of what others think of you. You will become more resilient. You will recognise the unique superpower that you bring to this world and you will believe that anything is possible for you. Because it is.

When you truly believe this, you will have the courage to take action in pursuit of your dreams. You will have an absolute conviction that your worthiness and your enoughness are not determined by what you do, but already an integral part of who you are.

I have always believed that every single woman already has the seeds of greatness inside of her and that includes you. All you need is the right environment and the right support to empower and inspire you to grow and this is why I launched **Flourish** in 2021.

All my coaching programmes are built on the same foundations as I have shared with you in this chapter – those of knowing and trusting yourself deeply and completely. Without these strong and resilient roots in place living a life of purpose, abundance and joy will always be out of reach.

I also understand how overwhelming it can feel to begin to unpick the beliefs and habits of a lifetime. Having the support, guidance, and encouragement of a coach can be an absolute game-changer. It can make you feel less alone. It made me realise that other women had faced the same limiting beliefs and self-sabotaging habits that I was experiencing and they had overcome them and if they could, then I could too.

I now have the honour of supporting other women through their journey to Flourish. When I work with coaching clients and we begin to explore the life they want to create it usually comes down to 3 core areas. They want to feel that they are living a life of purpose, that there is a sense of fulfilment, achievement, and success. They want to have the freedom to make choices in their lives; often they desire an abundance of time, energy, and money. They also want to feel ultimate happiness, to feel full of joy.

The truth is; purpose, achievement, fulfilment, success, freedom, choices, abundance, happiness and joy mean different things to every single one of us. They can't be attained by following someone else's plan or someone else's blueprint. Instead, the only way they can be a reality in your life is if you get super clear on what these words truly mean to you and what having these things in your life would look like and feel like for you. Only then can you identify what is keeping them out of your reach.

Along my journey of self-discovery, I have been so fortunate to have the opportunity to work with incredible women from across the other side of the world. To learn about their values, passions, and priorities in life and to help them gain clarity on what living a life of purpose, abundance and joy mean to them.

In reality, many of us don't know when we first begin on our journey to Flourish. We may have a vague awareness of what makes us happy or what financial abundance would look like for us, but it's not until we take the time to get to know ourselves that we get crystal clear.

For me getting crystal clear on who I am, what matters to me most, and what I want my life to look and feel like led me to stop constantly doubting myself and instead trust my intuition. I pivoted away from a business that no longer felt aligned, retrained as a life coach and launched my coaching business. As I have learned to truly embrace all aspects of me, my relationship with my partner has also grown. I am learning to communicate more effectively with him about how I feel, what triggers me and how he can best support me. In all areas of my life, I now place value on ease and flow, over hustle and burnout. Learning to set boundaries and follow what 'feels' makes life more joyful. I have learned that by taking the time to prioritise myself and my desires and needs I have an incredible opportunity to model the life I want my children to have. I want them to have an abundant and joyful and purposeful life and the best way that I know to teach them how to do this for themselves is to show them. To show them the value of prioritising themselves, getting to know who they truly are, and trusting their intuition. I know many of the women I work with feel the same:

- The woman who discovered her self-worth and left a relationship that was causing her more pain than joy now gets to create a life of security, love, and abundance.

- The woman who trusted her instincts and left the grind of the corporate world to find more fun, playfulness, and fulfilment.
- The woman who let go of her beliefs around money, overcame debt and launched a business from a place of passion and alignment. She now teaches others how to replicate her success and generate £10K+ months by following their joy.

Your life can be a success story too.

You already have the power within you to create an unlimited life of purpose, abundance, and joy. The answer has been within you all along. My wish for you is that you take what I have shared and that you have the courage to begin, the courage to look within. I promise that if you do you will finally recognise your true brilliance. You will unlock your untapped potential. You will make space for miracles in your life and your big dreams will become a reality.

You deserve to feel fulfilled, to live on purpose, and to live an inspired life. You deserve to feel excited, confident, and optimistic about your future. You deserve to thrive, to have an abundance of time, energy, and money. You deserve to **Flourish**.

If my story resonates with you and you feel called to connect it would be my pleasure and my honour to support you on your journey to **Flourish.** I'd like to take this opportunity to invite you to join my free community 'You Deserve To Flourish', where you can be the first to know about my latest offerings, connect with other like-minded souls and receive support and guidance. You can find us on Facebook at: www. facebook.com/groups/youdeservetoflourish/

You can also gain access to my latest FREE resource and join my email list by visiting: www.youdeservetoflourish.com

I currently offer:

- **121 Coaching -** a personalised 12-week immersive and transformational journey (You Deserve to Flourish) perfect if you are ready to deep dive and create radical change in your life.
- **Group coaching** - great for you if you are committed to change and want to feel supported and connected to other women on a similar journey

There are many other exciting opportunities on the horizon – watch this space!

If your intuition is calling you to explore working with me, please feel free to get in touch via email.

Love and Light, Lorraine

ABOUT THE AUTHOR

LORRAINE DAVIES

Lorraine Davies is a certified and accredited Life Coach who helps female entrepreneurs create an unlimited life of purpose, abundance and joy.

Lorraine has been successfully coaching and mentoring business owners since 2012. After growing a business and ranking within the top 3% of leaders in a network marketing company she decided to launch her coaching brand, **Flourish**.

As a Life Coach, Lorraine is an expert at helping mumpreneurs and female entrepreneurs recognise and realize their potential by tapping into their intuition, aligning their energy and taking inspired action.

Lorraine is known for her infectious energy and enjoys reading, gardening, yoga and movies.

Lorraine is available for coaching, mentoring and speaking engagements.

You can reach Lorraine at:

Email: lorraine@youdeservetoflourish.com
Website: www.youdeservetoflourish.com

 facebook.com/ldaviesvp

instagram.com/ldaviesvp

RED FLAGS AND OSTRICHES - BREAKING THE TRANCE OF DENIAL

MARIA ANTONETTE

DEDICATION

This chapter is dedicated to my son, my redeemer, Remy Emmanuel. I give thanks and praise to our creator for you. Remember son, never settle and always take bold life moves because inner contentment only arises when you honor your needs. Mommy loves you and will always be with you. I carry you in my heart, my amour infini.

How's my boo-boo doing today? He's doing okay, hip hip hip hooray!

> "You need to reach an inflection point. Without an inflection point there can be no change."

The pastor belted out. Arms raised, back arched, shirt buttons buckling against the weight of his ample, protruding belly. I remember this day so well, December 12, 2021.

WITHOUT AN INFLECTION POINT THERE CAN BE NO CHANGE

An inflection point is a turning point and I had experienced one. My inflection point found me on November 10, 2021, at 10:54am as I lay on my bed crying my heart out. I cried so hard that day, I felt my stomach would fall out. I remember the date and exact time because a week earlier I had learned of video journaling. This was my second time trying it. Along with a few other rescue remedies, video journaling freed me from an unbearable existence where I always felt alone and forgotten, further decline in my mental health and yet another crisis call to the local emergency department. *There's something about recording yourself on a video while crying, pleading, and baring your soul.*

On that insightful day in November, I cried a different cry, like I was mourning myself. I remember holding my stomach, crying out and saying, "This has to change, this has to change, I can't live like this anymore, please help me, Lord.' My marriage of 17 years had reached its end more than a decade ago, but it continued to drag on. It's presence creating a permanent reminder of failure. I could no longer pretend, no longer deny that I was living an unfulfilled existence.

I've watched that video back several times since. I look at the woman, the wife staring back at me with deep despair and sadness in her eyes and I don't recognize myself. But it was me. It was.

In 2021 I finally gave in to the small voice inside my head. At last, I faced the reality of my crushed emotions, dented self-worth, crippling fears, and deep inner sadness. This is the year I found the courage to leave my marriage.

I'd taken myself on a self-discovery journey in 2020. It started when I began my virtual paint party business Art by Journi2u during the Covid-19 worldwide pandemic. My confidence started growing and I was so proud of how my love of art brought people together at that perilous time. In 2021 I honed in on my need to reach people by starting a life coaching certification and accreditation course and celebrated my 50th birthday. I celebrated myself in the boldest way I knew how – by myself. I met a professional photographer at a beautiful retreat location I'd booked and 425 photographs later, I was sold – on myself and on my journey. As a result of my self-discovery journey, my spirit could no longer allow me to wither away *behind closed doors, in plain sight.* On that pivotal day in November, my soul spoke to me.

Let's fast forward to where I am now. Today, an unseasonably warm day in February 2022. I'm drinking a honey lavender herbal tea, crossed legged and sporting a bad hair day. My son is at school and I'm feeling at peace in this moment. The life I'm living now is unrecognizable. Do I mean, I'm covered in riches, languishing in natural spring waterfalls, being fed grapes by handsome Adonis like beings?

No.

But the life I lead now is richer than rubies, finer than silk and better than best. I'm cultivating a life that suits me. A life that suits Maria. The riches I'm experiencing are time to heal, self-love and faith. Nowadays, I am living life intentionally.

SEVENTEEN

As a young girl I was a shy, quiet, unassuming loner. I grew up with my three sisters and parents in Enfield, Middlesex, United Kingdom. Home life was hard at times especially with my dad dishing out corporal punishment - but that was a Jamaican thing.

I was a good kid, all my siblings were, but strict parenting caused a great deal of upheaval and after a disagreement with my Dad at aged 17, I was told to leave and to not return. *(Red Flags wave wildly here. Baby Ostriches are born).*

For me, this is when I started to feel like it was me against the world. That I must rely on myself to achieve, myself for stability, myself for finances, myself for EVERYTHING. But it was also a time that my self-talk of, "You're not worthy, not enough, insignificant, not treasured and you don't belong anywhere," came about. Working, struggling to pay bills, and living with a bunch of young girls all fighting to make it - was my new life. (*I wish I had known back then to tell myself, 'Maria you are doing the best you can with the knowledge that you have – you don't need to belong – create your own trail*). Forwarding through the years I bought my first property at aged 26 and left UK to head to America at aged 33 to marry and start a new life. If I had learned 'home is within me' sooner, I would have saved myself a world of anguish.

Please highlight this and meditate on it: Home is within me.

In the UK I remember climbing, ascending, and growing. Of course, I stumbled and made mistakes for several years but that was par to the course. I had a small network of friends, decent jobs and my wonderful flat. I traveled extensively, mainly to the Caribbean and Europe and am so happy I did it when I could. I often visited the spa, comedy clubs, dabbled in yoga and partied all weekend long for years and years. I always tried to enjoy life to the fullest. Back then I was never aware of my existence, never.

SECOND BEST

Settling for second best came naturally to me, especially in my love relationships. They had longevity, but they always seemed to like me, more than I liked them. You might wonder why I dated them. Remember the Ostrich and my need to belong?

This chapter is for you if you're rooted in your comfortable spot – you know the one that is comfortable yet brings pain, uncertainty, despair, and illness all wrapped up in denial? (Please read that again).

Here's an exercise for you:

Take a moment:

Close your eyes, take three long deep breaths with lengthy exhales.

Now is your time to acknowledge, plan, let go and grow. Say a silent prayer for strength and guidance.

> *Dear Lord/ Universe please direct my thoughts as I read this chapter. Help me to see my journey weaved between the lines.*

Provide me with the comfort and direction I crave. Inject courage into my mindset as I plan to welcome the best version of myself.

Amen.

Now grab a mirror. (I'll wait)

Look into your eyes and repeat after me, "I am ready to accept my story, to let go and grow."

Let's imagine for a moment I'm being interviewed by Oprah and you're in the audience (we can only dream):

Oprah: So, Maria, what do you think caused you to feel you weren't worthy, not enough, insignificant, and not treasured? What made you lose your sense of belonging, security, stability as a young woman?

Me: As I reflect on my life, I think the causes are threefold.

1. Not being as close as I needed to be with my Mum growing up *(thankfully our relationship changed for the better in my forty's).*
2. I have realized that my dad forcing me to leave my childhood home set the stage for how I felt my relationships should pan out. I remember always waiting for the relationship to end suddenly.
3. But ultimately not having the awareness to realize that I belong to myself did the most damage.

Because I have learned we can only do the best we can with the knowledge we have at the time, I have forgiven my parents wholeheartedly.

Oprah: Understood. Why did you stay so long in a marriage which no longer served you?

Me: I lived in denial (that my marriage was less than perfect) and I had become fearful of my ability to survive on my own. Yet, I also lived in hope. The denial also served to assist me in making myself believe there was hope, year after disappointing year.

Oprah: What gave you the courage to leave your marriage?

Me: Glow Society allowed me to self-actualize through their online coaching course and in turn gave me my wings.

Oprah: Wow, this is big. Could you tell me more about Glow Society?

Me: Definitely.

Let's move on.

I arrived in Atlanta, Georgia, USA on December 31, 2003. This was to be a new chapter for me, starting afresh, starting anew. *(Red flag. Time for another rug to be pulled)*. In 2004 I discovered I was pregnant. My response was panic and dread. Not the normal way for a woman to react considering this would be her first child, right? My reason being that I had experienced a life-threatening ectopic pregnancy at aged 27 In the UK:

Thinking back – it was a regular day, Summer 1998. My fiancé at the time was driving me to work. I worked at a slick publishing agency in Islington, North London, UK, and I loved it. Anyway, the first pain I felt, wasn't too bad. But the second? The second, made me lose my breath. The Lord's prayer came to me instantly. My fiancé got me to the hospital in what felt like minutes.

I will never forget in the ultrasound ward, as I lay there processing the news, I heard a young nurse assistant say, "Why is she crying?" The response, "She wanted her baby.' Overhearing that conversation forced me into quick acceptance, yet fuzzy denial. The days that ensued came and went; I wasn't a part of any of it.

Back to 2004 panic and dread: my mind whirled with every memory of Summer 1998. I wasn't excited about being pregnant, I was panicked, I was fearful, I was hopeful, I was newly married, and I wanted my baby, but a few weeks later I was told, "Sorry, Maria, you are experiencing an ectopic pregnancy, we need to prep you for surgery."

I remember feeling so empty, here I go again. At the hospital, the tears rolled from my eyes in a continuous stream, pooling inside the crease of my hospital gown. I sat in the bed, day after day disappointed, desperate, and alone. The nurses kept asking, "Why don't you have any visitors?" Except for one visitor who came wearing a 'World's best Dad' cap – the irony - I didn't know anyone. In hindsight, I asked myself, could being a loner from an early age have prepared me for this emptiness? I often thought about how leaving my family, friends, career, home, familiar surroundings, smells, and views, was a huge mistake.

I'd picked out a name this time, Journi Elise.

Being in a new country with no familiarity took a toll on me. I felt lonelier than I had ever felt. But a strange mixture of commitment, pride, denial and learned behavior kept me rooted in this reality. *(Ostrich)*. After my second ectopic pregnancy, I developed a racing heart. The stress I was under trying to acclimatize was immense. My days were long and arching. If only I had known what I know now. (*If only I had known I was at the helm, I was the driver, I had the ability to steer myself into acceptance, home was within me.*) Countless trips to the doctor ensued, depression pills prescribed (never taken), long nights lying awake, looking at the ceiling, many days smiling, while crying inside. Take a note of this quote:

> '*We suffer when we chase a dream or life that doesn't belong to us.*'
>
> — CAROLINE MYSS

When my immigration papers finally came through, I landed a job quickly, paid bills, made acquaintances, and tried to fit in and be.

Thought bubble: As I think a little deeper, I see why I've always settled for second best from men. The mixture of losing my security at an early age and feeling rejected, created a passive-submissive way of being. Leaving the UK and all I knew and loved rendered me even more vulnerable. So, I sought acceptance and security in a more fervent fashion. I was always trying to retrieve what my Dad had inadvertently taken from me. I wanted to belong somewhere. I wanted to feel necessary to a male figure, so as I started my new life in a strange country, I chose to relinquish the tight hold I'd built on independence and surrender to my marriage. But I had attracted the wrong energy into my life. What I know now is that I never needed to belong to anything or anyone. I already belonged to myself and all I ever needed was already inside of me.

My friend – the seeker, as you read on try to actively listen by focusing on your reactions, listen to your gut. Please remember grace and compassion, a gift we can always give ourselves.

In 2007 I discovered the news again that I was pregnant. You could hear a pin drop, but I embraced the news. I mean how unlucky can one gal get. I started a journal and allowed myself to breathe a little, envisioning the pitter patter of tiny feet.

But the news I received a few weeks later burst my bubble. "Maria, I'm sorry but you're experiencing a miscarriage."

Weariness set in. I told myself I do not deserve to be a mother, that I would probably abuse my child/children. I believed this was the reason I was being denied the privilege. Experiencing the fading pregnancy symptoms were the worst, the pain in my breasts started fading, the sickness subsided.

As I stood in my large walk-in closet (in my new home), punching my lower stomach with both fists. I remember saying, "If you don't want to stay inside of me, get out." That day will be permanently etched in my mind. I've never shared this. My dreams were plagued with nightmares, with images of babies with blue faces. Now, as I am so close to complete healing and as I live my purpose to serve others, it is my duty to share, to release.

So, in 2007, I would say I was numb. The feeling that won over everything, that knocked down all other contenders, was the denial. *(Ostrich)*. I've lived in a state of denial for most of my life.

In 2012, I discovered I was pregnant again. I had turned 40 years old. This time, I went to my knees in prayer, surrendering to the Lord. At 3 months pregnant, I felt that my pregnancy was confirmed, at this point I knew that my prayers had been answered.

My son Remy Emmanuel was born.

I've never felt such joy. (*Green flags and flamingos lol.*) A lot of thought went into his name. Remy is a French name which means remedy or laborer (I linked this to labor of love). His middle name is Emmanuel which means, God is with us. My son means the absolute world to me, his presence gives me power, motivation, courage, and strength. I love him more than words could ever describe. I got a tattoo when he was about 6 months old. It reads, 'Remy amour infini.' Universe: I send gratitude out to his father.

My friend – the seeker, please know that the Universe has your back. If there is something that you want, believe it to be yours. All I ask is for you to understand that it will never be your timing, but you must press on.

Enter: **Becoming aware of my existence**

SELF-BETRAYAL

Prior to my 2021 flight from my marriage, I had tried to leave before in 2015. However, three months later I returned for the sake of my son. I remember the night before I went back home, I had a terrible panic attack. (I ignored my intuition – she tried so hard, bless her). If she had a voice she would have said, "Maria, how long this time?"

In the forthcoming months I suffered immensely. *(Huge red flag, waving wildly)* Severe Depression, Generalized Anxiety Disorder, Panic Attacks, Suicidal Ideology and Post Traumatic Stress Disorder. The weight of my denial and self-betrayal was starting to show cracks. Frequent 911 calls, significant weight loss, insomnia, partial scalp numbness, inner head to toe body vibrations, face pain, malnutrition, nausea and vomiting, repetitive negative thoughts, terrifying mental pop-up visions (when I closed my eyes, I would see demonic visions – this was probably the most scariest affliction of them all – this is when I felt I was losing my mind) dizziness, neck aches, jaw aches and leg weakness were beacons of evidence that my environment did not serve me. I was crumbling. This was another extremely lonely time in my life. *(The Ostrich burrows deeper, but this time the red flag is wrapped tightly around its neck)*.

An excerpt from my journal in 2021 as I reflected on my past: *I let life happen to me by being passive and submissive, I didn't love myself.*

Seeing this written down has a sobering effect on me. I had been living, yet dying. There is no other way to describe the hell I went through during the first half of 2016. Looking at my young son and feeling like a failure, believing that my dream to become his Mommy was wasted on me, seeing life through panicked eyes, palpitations, and night terrors. At this time, because I had not shared the depths of my sickness and mental health decline, friends and family turned their backs because I could no longer stick to my promises and appeared flaky and unreliable. Ring any bells?

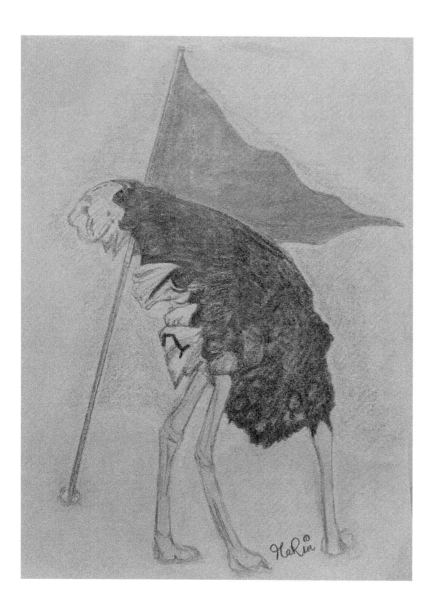

MY SAVING GRACE

Eckhart Tolle - spiritual teacher and self-help author. Talking about his book will always fire me up. I found it in a closet in

2016. The only reason I picked it up was because it was a bright orange color. It stood out. I cannot be any more grateful for A New Earth - Awakening to your life's purpose. The little orange book that calmed my tortured mind and spirit. I will be forever grateful that my steps were directed and this book was placed in my hand.

COURAGE

The foundation work took two years but my leap of faith; seconds. On November 16, 2021, at 11:29am, six days after my inflection point, I jumped out of my hammock and into the car with my son.

I made it! I put me first and the feelings surrounding my efforts are indescribable. The leap I took was in blind faith but in hindsight there was no alternative.

I've been there. I've sat in the muck and smelled the feces. I know what it's like to feel trapped and unsupported and unseen. I know it when I see it in others too. My joy for life started late, I don't want that for you, I want to open your eyes. It's time to stop living your life as a bystander and betraying yourself. If you get nothing else from my chapter, please take away that your intuition will save you – you need to tune in. Listen to your feelings, they won't lie. They will stir up in your gut. Notice when you get dietary issues and anxiety – big sign. Ask yourself often, "Does this feel good for me?" Danielle La Porte can guide you to recognize *good* with her book The Desire Map.

I truly believe that taking myself out of my natural surroundings contributed to my deep connection with the

Ostrich. Burying my head in the sand provided a safe place for me. A good coaching question is, "Does it serve you to stay stuck?" What do you think my answer would have been? Thankfully, I don't live with regret; I live with acceptance.

Enter my 2021 movement Journi2u. Birthed through my journey to me. I've started pursuing my business goals more courageously. My social media posts have become bolder, my photos show real confidence. I'm officially celebrating my beauty, my brand, me. I take boss moves now, bold strides and move like a lion, (roar) strong, steady, and courageous. I adopted a theme tune; Love Yourself by Mary J. Blige and created a playlist named 'Unleashed.' They empower me and are constant reminders that I am strong, and I can overcome.

My friend, the seeker, do you see yourself in my life story? What has resonated with you so far? Are you ready to take a step toward change?

I guide my clients to ignite a courageous and intentional life-style. To look in the mirror and talk to themselves, to look past the imperfections, to peel back the layers and see the child looking back. I get them to give their inner child what they need and then change the perspective and look back from their future self viewpoint.

A FREE GLIMPSE INTO MY INTENTIONAL SELF-DISCIPLINE WORKSHOP

Get yourself paper and a pen: Let's look at your life right now.

What do you need to change? Take. Your. Time.

Take a moment right now to list your desires, needs and wants. Look again at your list from your inner child perspective, then as the older you. Does your list suit all three of you? Who wasn't happy with what and why? Take the time to know yourself from every viewpoint. Now close your eyes and feel into your gut reactions (place your hand on your lower belly) Is the decision you are about to make the right one? How will you know if it isn't? Yep, you've got it – your stomach will feel unsettled. It's only by focused self-reflection that we come to know exactly what we need and when we need it.

REMEDIES

Finding myself during years 2020 – 2022 allowed me to break the trance of denial and self-betrayal. If I never do anything courageous again, my moves in 2021 will always hold the flag. I've learned that I am a warrior. I choose to be a peaceful warrior because that suits me and the tranquility that I have attracted into my world now. I love how empowered that makes me feel when I envision myself as She-Ra with heart.

This chapter has enabled a walk down memory lane for me. At times I've felt the emotions again, especially when I realized I hadn't dealt with the collective loss of three sweet babies. But with the tools I have acquired in the past few years I feel equipped to take on the world. She-Ra!

Do you want to see my weapons, my rescue remedies, what I use as add-ons to my 1:1 four pillar coaching program? They have never failed me or my clients. My tool bag of remedies and potions soothe heavy days when life's valleys appear. I am going to share three of the most powerful tools I have in my arsenal. These tools have consistently provided my clients with comfort, support, emotional release, and relief.

The first one makes me smile as I think about it:

QIGONG

A system of coordinated body-posture and movement, breathing, and meditation used for the purpose of health, spirituality, and martial-arts training.

I do not think I can express how greatly Qigong has helped my clients and I. I honestly do not have the words. What I can say is it is a bona fide rescue remedy. The various body movements, the shaking and the focusing inwards provide miracles. As soon as the 30-minute exercise is over, clients report that their nausea disappears. There is always an energy shift. I recommend this for anyone plagued with the heavy brain cloud and stomach complaints brought on by anxiety and depression. And for those who often feel 'off' or uneasy.

My second rescue remedy is extremely powerful too:

VIDEO JOURNALING

If you're not ready for change, don't mess with it. Remember what initiated my first inflection point?

As a result of my life's experiences, I trained myself to compartmentalize my emotions. I have often thought this was a good thing, but in times of emotional distress unable to shed tears, it became a big issue for me. I have found that video journaling brings on the tears. I have never had a problem with releasing my emotions since I found video journaling. Neither have my clients.

The next time you feel 'off,' or feel voiceless, press record, and start talking. Tell me how you get on.

The third, but not the last:

SOUND BATHS

No, this doesn't include water unless of course you want to jump in the tub while listening…(recommended). The sound I am particularly aligned with is 741 hz and Tibetan singing bowls are my goto. The melodious sounds they emit send a message to your soul (in my humble opinion). If you want to rid yourself of negative energy, toxins, or experience a spiritual awakening, try a sound bath. I use these for clients who feel 'off', lonely, emotionally and physically tired or exhibit signs of overwhelm. I use candles, distraction free environments and a few other choices to bring favorable results.

My tool bag is full of so many goodies, they've helped me to achieve mastery of my emotions and I share whenever I can. Want one? There's more where these came from.

Red Flags and Ostriches please rest now or find comfort in one another but leave me the heck alone.

REFLECTIONS AND THANKS

When I made the bed this morning, I was called to look up at the crisp white cotton sheet billowing in the air. In that moment I felt such a sense of peace, *in the space between the sheets*. That was my second inflection point – complete inner peace beckons.

Thank you 2020 for helping me to learn what self-love is. Now that I love myself, I am safe in the knowledge that toxic environments, neglect, rejection, criticism, guilt trips, narcissistic and emotional abuse have no place in my life. I fiercely protect my peace and no longer live the passive, "It's okay" and the hopeful, "Things will get better" toxic lifestyle. There is still a journey to take in my world, and I'm ready.

Thank you, to the stranger who hugged me as I was leaving the hospital after my second ectopic. I will always remember her kind touch, her touch of love.

Thank you JT for your generosity and for holding space.

My friend – the seeker, please answer anxiety's call – she's on your side. Please listen to the tiny voice inside you, you must be still to hear it. I recently took the time to listen and what I heard will stay with me forever, "Your boat will not break." Thank you, Jesus.

LET GO & GROW

Affirmation: I love me and I accept all that has happened, because it happened for me not too me. I accept all of the good that is coming my way with a wide smile and open arms.

My friend – the seeker, I love you for your potential, your courageousness, and your bravery for realizing that you are enough.

Do you feel called to become a Journi warrior? My coaching program is for:

Those who have awoken and need rescuing, who betray themselves, who live in denial, who settle for second best, who are dying on the inside while smiling on the outside.

If your marriage no longer serves you, let's work on a way out and put our energy towards attracting better. If your job no longer serves you, let's open doors to a more aligned one. If your best friend has morphed into your enemy, let me help you to move on, work on yourself and attract better connections. If self-sabotage visits you frequently, let's say goodbye together. Whatever you need to let go of, know that it can be done. Let's continue to build on our empowered and unleashed community.

As a certified and accredited practitioner coach, my coaching program, Intuition – The Truth allows you to self-actualize and let go and grow through a focus on motivation and courage. Hand crafted 'Unique2u' modalities and nurturing motivational healing techniques equip you as you grow.

I know that investing in self is daunting, especially if you're not used to it. But investing in self shows you've recognized your worth. Nothing is more powerful than someone who knows their worth.

The time has come to grab your sword and shield my friend.

Now Charge!

ABOUT THE AUTHOR

MARIA ANTONETTE

Maria is a certified and accredited intuitive life coach who utilizes expressive arts and healing techniques to ignite self-promotion and courage consistency in her clients. As a freelance artist she expresses herself through acrylics on canvas.

It took Maria two focused and intentional years to find herself, her strategy recorded and transformed into a powerful coaching program. Her let go and grow blueprint lightens the load for those who journey with her.

Maria spends her time enriching her relationship with her son, honing personal development and sun worshipping (beach anyone?). She's known for her smile, dry humor, peaceful demeanor and drive.

Maria is available for coaching and commissioned art consults.

You can reach Maria at:

Email: Journi2u@gmail.com
Facebook: https://bit.ly/Journi2u
Website: Journi2u.com
Blog: https://whatshesaidart.wordpress.com/
https://linktr.ee/Art_by_journi2u for Journi2u workshops and more.

instagram.com/journi2u_courage

LIVING FROM THE INSIDE-OUT

SILVANA DA SILVA

My finances were beginning to run thin, and I was faced with the ultimate decision. Do I continue this downward spiral, or do I take the unfamiliar path of going within not knowing what I might uncover? The former hadn't worked for me up until now and I was so desperate that I chose the latter.

To the outside world, I had it all. By my early twenties, I was in a management position, lived in my own home, had a flashy car, was always presentable, and had a partner who was driven and ambitious. I was the definition of what a successful and happy woman should be. But when the curtains were drawn, the story was entirely different on the inside. If only the outside world knew of my financial struggles, and how truly unhappy and unfulfilled I was within myself and my relationship. I knew even then those superficial things were not the true measure of my life or all that I wanted to experience during my time on earth.

I was inspired to take the journey within by my mother who had begun her own self-discovery transformation. As my mum was clearing out cobwebs from her past, she handed me a CD from Louise Hay of positive daily affirmations, and my very own copy of The Secret. I began soaking it all in. I created my own vision board and personalised affirmations. And for the first time in a long time, I began to feel peace and confidence in how my future would turn out. I felt at home and comforted when I created and worked on myself. I knew my dreams were bigger than my current reality.

The journey inside of myself was lonely at times, but it never felt like a sacrifice only a world of unlimited possibilities.

Now some 10 years on, my vision board has become my reality. I am grateful for the lows, the lessons, and the pain, for these, truly were my biggest blessings and redirections to the path that was intended for me. I now live in all manners of abundance because I chose to listen when my soul was asking me to.

To the woman you have been, the woman you are now, and the woman you are yet to become, your faith in the unknown has and will always be your biggest asset.

To all my success, I owe it to my mother who taught me to think outside of the box and inspired me with her own journey.

I was the first generation in my family to own a pair of shoes as a birthright. My family came from humble beginnings in a remote village on the island of Madeira, Portugal. My mum was born in a stone-built shed where hay bales were for beds and had to leave primary school early to work on the farm. I tell you this as it played a significant part in my upbringing and beliefs.

My father was absent growing up and my mum was twenty when she had me, frowned upon for not following traditional norms we moved to the UK when I was two years old. My first memories were of feeling abundantly loved and protected by my mum, but I could sense her sadness and desire to create a better life for me than she had for herself. It was just the two of us and my mum worked relentlessly. She leaned on me as much as I leaned on her for strength and support to keep going, in the hope of better days.

I grew up with the same resilience towards work and fierce independence to make something of my life. I inherited the belief that no work was easy and required great sacrifice, that money was hard to acquire and left effortlessly. There was always a desire to prove people wrong at the end. To be that underdog who accomplished what others thought was not possible or reasonable.

I certainly wasn't academic, and I recall a teacher even telling me so. I was the creative kind and all I really wanted to do was work and so I started at the age of 14. With my weekend work, I would cover my costs for school food, transport, and a little extra. Years later I would go on to drop out of university after a month and pick up a full-time job instead. Every year or two after that I moved up in job role and salary. I never stopped until I hit the age of 28, I had bought my second home and was on 50k without a single degree under my belt.

At this stage, I knew I had gone as far as I wanted to in my corporate career and there was still so much I wanted to accomplish. I wanted to give back to women who were going through similar journeys, those who started with the basics and wanted to create an exponential life for themselves and their families. Women who wanted to rewrite the pain from their family's past and inherited beliefs. Most importantly I wanted to help women create the life they want on the outside without neglecting their own needs on the inside – their true essence.

Without the knowledge and awareness of what was going on inside of me, I do not believe I would be where I am today, living my vision board and defying my perceived limitations. There are moments when I wish I had known a coach who could have helped me during all my struggles, but in all honesty, 12 years ago I do not even think that was an option for me. Instead, I had a mentor, I had my mother teaching me the ropes and the latest self-development tools. I know now that my journey was to experience the pain firsthand, apply the tools, and figure out what worked and what did not, so that I may share this with fellow women.

I was always a nurturer, a caregiver, an empath and so I knew for many years my passion was people. Even though my energy was quite masculine in the corporate world, it was this feminine side of me that set me apart and often raised eyebrows.

It was 8 years ago when I first resonated with the concept of becoming a women's coach and mentor during an energy reading seminar. I was twenty-two and first discovered the difference between my ego and my intuition. This was all a lot to take in in your early twenties when you think you know it all! I remember resisting the suggestion that everything I had experienced I had created, "What? I am responsible for everything that has happened to me. I have sabotaged my own experiences, no way I wanted it so badly. There is no way I would have wanted that result!" The hardest pill to swallow was learning that which you wanted so dearly you managed to push away purely based on what you believed you deserved. The second hardest pill to swallow is that you cannot change or mold anyone to suit your needs and desires, no matter how good your intentions are.

I started to realise how the most widely held belief of us all "I am not good enough" had shown up in my life repetitively. The constant need for validation from partners resulted in being cheated on and undermined only reaffirming this belief. The "I'm not worthy" flared up when I would get passed up on the work promotion. The "Perfectionist" who was scared to show up as her true authentic self in case it was not perfect enough. I was never able to be or feel authentic or vulnerable which limited so many experiences in my life and left me with the real what if's. I understood then that I would either allow my beliefs to limit and dictate the rest of my life or I could become aware of them and when they showed up.

I decided to take control.

Now let me set the record straight, becoming aware of your beliefs does not offer a quick-fix solution, and suddenly you are firing from all cylinders. Like anything, it takes time and practice, trial, and error but what happens is greater than you could ever expect. You really get to know yourself. You honour who you are, you trust your journey, and you become your own best friend. Yes, you may nag yourself occasionally like you would a friend but at the end of the day, there is nothing there but an utmost love and appreciation for who you truly are, believing in your journey, and knowing that you are only ever trying your best. This was the link that I had been missing.

What I thought I wanted back then was for someone to offer exact instructions on how I could save my relationship and make more money and that would fundamentally equal my happiness. So, I set out on a new self-development workshop. In all honesty, I was quite disappointed that no one was going to sit me down one-to-one and listen to all my woes. I wanted someone to save me whilst I was trying to save others, could a more ironic desire exist? But now I had taken in all the knowledge from seminars, books, and audios and I was ready to apply a real change in my life!

A couple of months after starting my self-development journey, my partner of 3 years vanished without a word, I had left my job after continuous bullying, I had no money, and had to move out of my home. I felt defeated. Everything I had ever worked for was gone within a blink of an eye. This was the lowest point in my life. Every belief I had was being ultimately tested and my default response was to become the victim of circumstance, but now I had something even more powerful.

I had the tools that would not only fix one area of my life but every single part of it. I had the awareness of my beliefs and how they were showing up in my life, and even better, I had the gift of my intuition which I had learned to tap into at any moment to decide my future. I was now in control of how I responded to what happened to me and I could not have been tested anymore in the use of these tools than I was at that very moment.

I felt like I had gone from hero to zero. I switched off from everything else that was going on around me and I just went inside. I cried I screamed, I got angry, I felt exhausted, used, and betrayed but I knew I had to let it surface.

I moved back in with my mum and allowed the healing to take place. What I discovered was that I had always played it small. When it came to relationships, I did not feel like I deserved to be loved. My experience of love was that when you loved someone, they always left you. I saw it happen to my mum many times and assumed that was why my dad was never around. So, I dimmed my light in order to be everything my partners needed from me, after all, we all just want to be loved.

In being everything they wanted I lost myself. I could not even remember who I really was. What hobbies did I enjoy? What was my own dress sense? What was my opinion on matters? I remember feeling so insecure and frustrated. My mood would instantly switch if ever I felt like the love that I needed was in threat or inadequate. I was trying so desperately to search for something to fill the void inside of me, had I only known that the answer was always being reflected back to me, just in different faces.

The area that I always had the most control over was my career and making money. If I put my mind to something, you'd better know I was not giving up until I got it! But my need for acceptance would creep up here too. I would doubt my abilities when in senior meetings or speaking to someone with more authority. I was however able to detach from this more personally than I could in my relationships. I was jumping from promotion to promotion every year or two feeling like this was the only real part of my life I had some control over. With this came great sacrifice. I was missing out on those important family moments, neglecting my health, and any form of balance in my life. My only thought was to learn everything I needed to about this role and once I had achieved that I would be ready for the next leap. I poured in blood, sweat, and tears. I was well and truly stuck on the hamster wheel.

Life had very few pleasures or adventures that someone of my age should have been experiencing. I needed an identity and when my relationships failed my job gave me just that. All the while I kept on ignoring this nagging feeling that there had to be more to life, instead, I focused on work for a sense of purpose and security. It was a safety net in a world of unknowns. I recall that on the rare occasions I went out with friends or family I would for that moment just enjoy being alive. I had forgotten what my true laugh sounded like and that the important moments were not how well you performed in a meeting but in creating memories with the people you love. During the pain of my lowest moment, I realised everything in my life that held true value, and that I once paid little attention to, was what ended up saving me.

Within a few weeks of losing everything, I received a phone call for an interview. My confidence was shot but I had little left to lose, so I put on my best suit, a brave face, and went out into the world to try again. In short, they loved me. I got the job. The interviewer, who then became my manager and mentor for many years, saw something in me that I could no longer see. He believed in me when I no longer believed in myself. I do believe that angels come in all forms, and they show up in unexpected ways as we go through our healing journey. To him, I will always be grateful.

I slowly began to put the pieces of myself back together and had my wonderful mother beside me every step of the way. I tried to hide my pain from her because no mother wants to see their daughter's heart breaking, but she knew me better than I knew myself. I was ashamed and felt an obligation to protect my her, but I knew even if I did not say it, she would still sense it.

I wondered how such wonderful people could exist in a world where there were those who only caused you pain, I could not understand it because I could never do the same. Perhaps it was unintentional, maybe they were just cowards, or they were hurting too and didn't know how to express it, so they made others suffer. I was not sure if I should be angrier at those who caused me pain or at those who witnessed it and turned a blind eye. The first drove you crazy and the latter made you think you were actually crazy!

I would often dissect every part of what happened to me during this time. How did I go from being in my early twenties with my first property, a respectable job, and a partner I thought I would be with for life to what seemed like homeless, jobless, and alone? Oh, how the mighty had fallen! To make matters worse I had just attended a life-changing seminar before it all fell apart, surely things should have gotten better from there not worse! None of this made sense.

I hated the saying everything happens for a reason. You had to wait to get to the other side of all the heartache and pain to understand what that reason was. I wanted to know the reason NOW so I could get this over and done with, but life doesn't work that way. My mum still reminds me to this day that it is never really about the destination but the journey that takes you there. I wanted a quick fix solution but deep down I knew something far greater had to change, that I would have to grow through this moment.

It was day one of my new job and my new life. I had decided that from this darkness I was dedicated to changing the narrative of my life. I had wallowed in it; I had overthought every part of it and now I needed the cycle to stop. I had the choice to continue going through the motions and allowing life to happen to me or to step up and change my perspective. I already had the tools I needed, now I just had to apply them. I knew I had an underlying not-good-enough and unworthy belief and how these had played out in my life so far. All I had to do was wake up! To become aware of when these feelings crept up and to choose differently. I would say to myself "I am free from the past, free from the future and here in the now" take a deep breath, become present and follow through with my intuition. I practiced this process repeatedly. Every single day I focused on these two parts to get me through the day. Become aware of the belief and follow my intuition, rinse, and repeat.

I still had moments of mental weakness and self-torture, but this process kept me going as I healed slowly but surely. At times I still felt like a shell of myself but then I remembered I had already felt that way for so long. I had shown up how others wanted me to and so by default I was always going to fall back into that way of thinking and feeling. I learned to be patient with myself and to accept that I was figuring out a whole new way of living. With each new opportunity and potential trigger, I was tested. Sometimes I would fall victim to it, but you can be certain that the next time I would be onto it!

This became my new way of living. I remember feeling so empowered for the first time in my life, even though I had little in the outside world to show for it. I had never felt more connected to myself, more entrusting in my intuitive guidance. I recall feeling drained by the end of the day from all the additional focus I had to apply, but like learning a new job, the first few months are graft and suddenly it all becomes second nature. I would remind myself of how much more exhausting and disempowering it was to feel like all these things were happening to me, and how much time I would previously spend fixating on past incidents for hours if not days. Now I acknowledged moments when someone said something that tugged at my old beliefs, allowed the feelings to rise and decided to react differently. I would often look at the bigger picture. Perhaps they were just having a bad day, maybe they felt inadequate in their abilities and threw their weight around to compensate. Whatever their reason may have been, that was their journey and not mine. I would just let it go.

I felt liberated not only from the opinions of others but from my own self-doubt and judgment. I was living and making decisions from a place that felt powerful, aligned, and true to me. I began sensing my energy shifting now from inside me. What began as a mental task of "why has that offended me, that must have triggered my "I am not worthy belief" now became a sensation in my stomach, a form of tension. I no longer had to do the pedal work and simply knew when to shift my focus and energy.

I did this all in private, nobody else needed to know the internal journey I was going through. I did not need anyone ridiculing or undermining my journey all because they were not yet willing to embark on theirs. It takes a level of responsibility and accountability and a whole lot of guts to go within. Some people never do and that is okay too. I never pushed my ideas onto anyone who was not interested. Instead, I would let the work show for itself.

Today I write this chapter from my house in the countryside overlooking a valley. It has been 8 years since I began my new life, and since my life gained so much harmony and fluidity. Yes, I was still tested along the way. That is part of the process to allow for new and wonderful things to unfold.

I am engaged to a brilliant man and my best friend, we share a Doberman puppy – the apple of our eye! But most importantly I am happy, inside, and out.

I am grateful to the young woman who lost it all and decided to go within regardless of fear or judgment. She made today all possible.

I have created a life filled with love, finances, freedom, time, and businesses that I love.

Over the years that followed I continued to climb the ranks at work with confidence, ease, and always from a place of love. Once I reached the last job goal, I decided it was time to fulfill my life's purpose of guiding women to create and experience the same.

My relationships also improved and even in moments where others tried to compromise on my values or authenticity I began to choose otherwise and had the confidence to walk away. I became my own best friend and biggest supporter, and I trust myself with every ounce of my being. When encountering people who challenged me at work or personally, I kept the bigger picture in mind, a sense of empathy and I let it go. I did not always get it right, but I knew it was a journey, what mattered was acknowledging and committing to being better the next time.

I sometimes wonder how my life would have turned out if I did not have the tools and need for change. Would I still be seeking love outside of myself? Would I still be stuck in an unhappy relationship? There were moments when this could have become my reality. Would I be stuck in a state of depression and dissatisfaction at work? Maybe I would have gone too far the other way and not stopped working until I realised the better years had passed me by? This too could have become my reality. Perhaps I would have spent the rest of my life acquiring more and more luxury items whilst crippled by debt? These could all have been potential avenues for my time here on earth. I know it to be true because I can relate to the unhealthy beliefs that attract me to them.

I know now that my journey begins and will end with me. There is nothing in the outside world that will do that work for me. I was fortunate to have a source of inspiration to lead me on the right path when I felt called and ready to listen.

Most women do not embark on this journey until they feel ready to. I do not believe there is a right or wrong time to start. Our journeys are all different yet similar in ways. Once you really get to know yourself on the inside you will create miracles on the outside.

Once you have ironed out those beliefs which are sabotaging your happiness and life experiences, you move from the passenger to the driver's seat. You take control and your power back. As is said, "With great power comes great responsibility." The only question is are you ready to take responsibility? When you feel ready to dictate what you want from life you will discover that you already have all the answers you need inside of you, all that is missing is the key. You are the key, everything else is just a bonus.

In 2014 I journaled that my life's passion was to inspire and empower women. I had no idea how I was going to do it then. All I had was faith that it would unfold when and how it was meant to. Today I have an established coaching business and programs that I offer to fellow women who are currently going through or have just come out of their own low moments. It does not necessarily mean that anything significant has had to happen, some women just feel stuck on the hamster wheel and need help getting out - they desire a life filled with more meaning and substance.

Through applying the techniques I have personally tried, tested, and know to be true I help women uncover what is really holding them back. Often what we think is causing us to struggle and suffer is not always what it seems. I take women through a journey of divinity, to find peace within themselves and to create the life they long for. I do not believe that every two women are the same, even when backgrounds and childhoods are similar, we can be completely different from one another. I believe in getting to know my clients below the surface. I get to know their hearts. It is here that your true desires and unique piece of magic reside. Had this option been available to me back then it would have saved me many years of hard lessons, but I honour that it was this journey that enables me to support and inspire women today.

I know that we can decide to change our lives at any given moment. I know it because I have lived it. We can choose to live life as a victim or we can experience a divine awakening and create a life that reflects our joy. Every day does not need to feel like a struggle, but an exciting day filled with new opportunities, where you are in control. I have seen this in the women that I have had the pleasure to know and work with. An aha moment that explains a lifetime of patterns. Women who realise what they thought they wanted to achieve were only compensating for areas where they felt lacking. Your dreams are never too big or unrealistic if they are aligned with your greater good. How do you know if it is for your greater good? Go within. Does it bring you love, tears of joy, and freedom?

Some of my clients want to achieve wonderful things and give back to the world but thought the idea of having it "someday" would be nice. Why wait? You can start to take steps toward your desires right now no matter how small the task may appear, it is progress. The biggest gift I can ever impart to the women I work with is teaching them how to reconnect with who they truly are. To see them find the inner peace they have been seeking for so long. To find freedom from all their perceived limitations. I teach and watch as women become more patient and accepting of themselves, speak kinder to themselves, and let go of the need to judge every action they take. I watch their dreams unfold before their very eyes.

My greatest joy is to see a woman who has become lost find her way back home to herself, I remember that feeling so well.

There is no greater power than the love we can have for ourselves, both inside and out. If you can learn to reconnect with yourself life unfolds for you in ways you could never have imagined. Become aware of those beliefs and most importantly choose. Choose how you want every moment to play out in your life, will it be as the victim, or the empowered woman who resides within you. Divine awakenings do not happen overnight, however, once we resolve one area the same rule applies throughout life. I have guided and supported women through both professional and personal stress, financial strains, unhealthy habits, time management, poor relationships and so much more. All by using the same techniques.

If you ever question the direction of your life, know this is your divine wisdom telling you something is off balance. This is your intuitive nudge for change. You may try to drown it out as I did and for brief moments forget it is even there but as soon as the silence returns and the busy has gone, she will return to remind you. Your divine self only ever wants what is best for you. Always remember that. Unlike your beliefs or ego, she will never sabotage the wonderful experiences which are open to you right now!

If only we never lost that connection to her when we were young and carefree but along the way, we all do. We let the world dictate what we can or cannot do, and how we should or should not act. When all we really want to do is reconnect with the little girl we use to be who would burst into a room in full song, not caring if her gut was hanging out or her hair was all over the place.

She was fun, she was free, and she was happy. Isn't that all that we really want to feel? Do you feel it is time for you to reconnect to yourself? To become the author of your own story?

You can have it all. You can enjoy life and be excited about the journey ahead from a place of confidence and inner knowing that whatever happens, your divine self, your intuition, will always, and I mean always have your back, as will I.

I hope you have enjoyed reading, and if you would like to find out more about how I help women in achieving this high state of reconnection, I would love to hear from you. Add me on my socials and let's connect.

I also have a free online course on my website to help you find out how your limiting beliefs may be sabotaging your life experiences so that you may begin uncovering your true potential now.

All my love on your journey back to you.

Silvana x

ABOUT THE AUTHOR

SILVANA DA SILVA

Silvana Da Silva is an accredited coach & mentor with the IAPC&M specialising in Intuitive Living. She is also the Founder of Life Inside Out Ltd; a service and community for ambitious women who aspire to create an intuitive-lead life filled with harmony and ease.

Following her own turning point, Silvana decided it was time to create a safe and inspirational space for women who are ready to rediscover their divinity – their true selves. To experience on the outside what they desire on the inside.

Silvana has been coaching & mentoring women for 6 years and now delivers her all-encompassing 3 R's program to women who hear the calling.

Silvana has a fascination with seeing the true potential and beauty in everything and applies that within her property business too. Her highest values are laughter, love, and faith which you can expect to see in all areas of her life and work. During her free time, you will find her walking her pooch Lea, at the gym, or having a cheeky nap on the sofa.

If you need a shift in your life but fear what may that look like for you, Silvana will make you feel like you have always been lifelong friends. You can expect to feel safe, warm, loved, and appreciated – with a dash of dry humor too!

You can reach out to Silvana at:

Email – Silvana@lifeinsideoutltd.com
Website - https://lifeinsideoutltd.com/

 facebook.com/Silvana.lifeinsideout
instagram.com/Silvana.lifeinsideout

THE NEXT CHAPTER...

TERESA MURRAY

*Y*es, that is right. You're just about to start reading chapter two of my life.

What happened to chapter one, you might want to ask?

Well, this one I have written in a *There She Glows Volume Two* collaboration book. You are more than welcome to buy it and read it before this one. Or after. The choice is yours, and only yours, like everything else in this life. Only we are responsible for the choices and decisions we make.

The same choices that I have made in my life led me to where I am now. It wasn't easy but was totally worth it.

So, where am I now?

It took me many decisions to make, many courses to buy and do, many people - to meet and to great. And some of them to keep, and others to let go.

Every lesson I have learned, easy or hard way - gave me something to think about and gave me some more wisdom and knowledge. There is always something new to learn. And it always will be. It will come back, again and again, to learn, re-learn and keep up whatever it did not remember before.

Whatever lessons your *Soul* have not understood and didn't learn will carry it to another lifetime. Not in just this lifetime journey of one's *Soul*. Yes, You have read it right- *Soul lifetime journey*.

But first things first. How did I get where I am now and how my knowledge and wisdom can help you live and thrive?

I am sure you know that feeling where whatever you doing does not make you feel good? Or happy? Or seem that people do not understand you whatsoever? You feel lost and unfulfilled. You keep searching for that calling and can't find it as everything you do or how you live your life does not make you happy. Do not worry; there is nothing wrong with you. Or, in fact, there is nothing wrong with them. Your children- if you have any. Or nothing wrong with your better half, your parents, your friends. Nobody... We all have a purpose of fulfilling. Some of us feel it; others- don't.

Would it not be easier to know why they are the way they are? Learning how to talk to them or accept the way they are - would make your life and other people's lives so much easier, right?

What if I tell you that there is a way to know why you are the way you are? And why do you or others behave one way or another?

Live like you're gonna die tomorrow. Learn as if you gonna live forever…

I do not remember where or when I have heard this sentence, but it does stick with me. And it perfectly describes how I feel about finding my life purpose, digging deeper and deeper into what am I doing on this planet earth?

One day my dear friend popped in for coffee and started to tell me about Tarot cards. She was bragging about this fantastic course she was attending online. At first, I just asked her to do my card reading. I always was into some so-called woo woo stuff and occasionally would have my Tarot card reading done. When I have felt stuck. And needed some guidance or some questions to be answered.

At that point, I felt a little bit stuck. I was a kinda housewife. Due to a personal situation at home, I could not work elsewhere, just at home. And I wanted to know what my next step could or should be. Doing the same thing over and over - was not for me. I needed a change. And just needed some hint from Universe about what that could be.

In that card reading, my friend saw and told me that my life purpose is to lead others and share my wisdom. It was given to me to learn something magical, something spiritual and teach and help others. I thought then that I did not know enough to share with others. But aren't we all feeling the same? Does not matter how much we do know.

After a few weeks, I suddenly felt that I would love to learn tarot cards.

So, I have gone and registered for the same online course. And I have loved it. And still do.

Through the same esoteric institution, I have been invited for a short course called „ *Soul Formula in your life"*. It really intrigued me. What is that *Soul Formula* about? No, it is not a *Human Design*.

How many nights did the clear night sky show you the beauty of stars?

Have you ever read your horoscope and thought to yourself -„ It is total nonsense. It is not about me at all! "Well, of course, is it not correct.

Purely because the same month or astrological sing people can not be all the same. But to write up about each and everyone is impossible. There are so many factors that need to be looked at to be analysed.

We carry the *divine light* and wisdom of our ancestors in our souls. There are plenty of ways and tools to read, listen to, and know what messages are there for us or around us. We just forgot how to listen to our intuition and use it wisely.

I just love seeing, reading, and finding all the signs that Universe is sending my way.

There is nothing accidental in our life.

The Universe speaks to us in the language of the stars. We need to know how to read it. We all came to learn something at our life University.

I have been searching for myself. What is there for me in this lifetime? What lessons did my *Soul* come here to learn? What karmic baggage did it carry from a previous life?

Soul Formula's creator is Russian astropsychologist A.Astrogor.

Astropsychology - is a science of astrology and psychology together.

New cosmic psychology allows us to analyse the position of planets at a particular time of a person's time and place of birth, discovering what characteristics in life this person has and why it is behaving one way or another.

First of all, I wanted to know how it works. Luckily, me being multilingual, and I could do that in the Lithuanian language. So, I have done a short course on it.

And, oh boy - it blew my mind away!

> *"The Soul Formula takes us to the world of human destiny. To have their souls sing and get a new breath, for these souls to rise and help other souls to fly. Fly the way of life, not wander. For everyone to discover their place in life. To receive a dose of inspiration and never let it go again. And then things start to change in the life of those people who have heard."*
>
> — *A. ASTROGOR.*

Soul Formula is the quickest way to tell about a person, what they are like, and where they might be going. It is the fastest way of telling man's destiny and character.

Soul Formula can analyse life purpose, health, finances and business. It can help with having better relationships within a family, with children. With your loved ones or friends.

It can clarify why you love doing something that, for others, does not make sense.

Analysing *Soul Formula* can show better career choices. How to make the most of your hobbies and have the best holidays that you would really enjoy.

As astropsychologist A. Astrogor says, ***it is a God's stamp in a passport of our life, where our destiny, purpose and path of refinement are coded in***.

It does not need to do any tests or long and tiring consultations that would need to be repeated again and again. It is done easy and quick way and very informative.

By learning the formula for your *Soul*, you will gain more confidence in your life choices or know what needs to change to live in harmony with yourself.

This information provides guidelines for life. It is one of the most effective ways to learn your strengths and weaknesses, strengths and weaknesses of character, mission, vocation, temptations, and areas of success.

With the precise range of human compatibility, everyone can understand each other better. Everyone would be able to live by the scenario written in stars for them and would not feel lost and unfulfilled.

But then again - it is everyone's choice to live happily... or not...

In a *Soul Formula*, we can encode information about:

Health - possible disorders and ways to avoid them.

Finances - what threats, opportunities are there and how to get them.

Self-realisation- the most suitable professions, life mission, a path of improvement, successes and threats.

Relationships - with children, parents, partners, bosses, friends, colleagues, acquaintances, and everyone we would like to understand better.

Stars not just encourage us but make us do what is meant for us.

If you don't live by the energies of the planets given to you, you don't live to your full potential.

By changing our ways of thinking, we are changing our fate.

Knowing your purpose in your life - would not that make you feel great?

But, unless you actually go and really uncover your personal layers, you would only be able to understand who you are at that personal *Soul* level. Discovering your unique *Soul Formula* can give an answer to everything you have been looking and searching for. But do not expect that this will provide you with some magical sweet that you think you would just swallow, and all will happen. You still need to do the work.

Soul Formula - it is not future telling!

So, how does it work?

There are 10 planets & 4 fictitious points.

We all know *Sun, Moon, Mercury, Venus, Mars, Jupiter, Saturn, Neptune, Pluto, Uranus.*

Fictitious points are - *Selena* (white Moon), *Lilit* (black Moon), *North node & C*hiron key.

All this makes your Soul Formula chart. But most important is to look at the planets in the centre when you were born. It indicates what internals we have in us.

Every planet and a fictitious point has its energy.

For example, Sun - it is masculine energy. Venus - feminine energy. And so on. If planets are in the centre of your Soul Formula, their powers will be more vital than those in the other orbits.

For example, I will analyse a short version of my own Soul Formula so you have a grip on what it is all about.

There is a cosmogram, there is -,, **INDIGO CHILDREN"**. Of course, when I individually work with clients, it is much to be analysed and looked into, not just this. As well, as would need to look at planets in orbits too.

To better understand what it is all about and how it looks, I will analyse my own *Soul Formula*. Bear in mind- that it is just a short version of it.

Below you can see a picture of my Soul Formula.

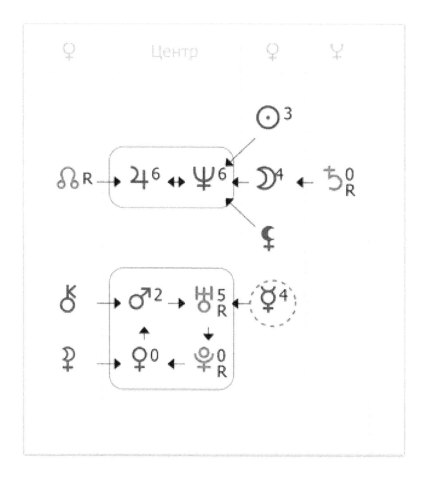

In my Soul Formula, I have two centres. Six planets altogether. It shows that I am very versatile and multi-layered. I have a lot going on in everything. I can realise myself in several areas. I most likely have, and it is good to have several activities and hobbies. If not, then that one activity should have some change so that there is no monotony. There may be some distractions, but it is essential to multitask as little as possible to try to focus on one action. If I choose to realise myself in several areas anyway, it is vital to choose one main activity and consider all the others as hobbies.

My first centre is the most important because here is also my karmic mission, which consists of Jupiter and Neptune. The mission- North node points specifically to Jupiter, but it still usually includes if there are other planets connected together. In my case - Neptune is with that Jupiter. Jupiter is a very social planet. I have a great sense of justice and moral standards. Planet energies indicate my generosity and that I am noble. Jupiter, this is the teacher. If I couldn't find a place to realise myself through training, I could become a great moraliser. Or would try to teach everyone everything and everything. This planet is so much expanding its horizons and thinking. Sometimes it can evoke a bit of a sense of pride. Jupiter is a very non-domestic planet. For me, the most crucial self-realisation is outside the home. Even when I was on maternity leave, I had to find an opportunity to work because sitting at home without some social activity made me very unhappy. Jupiter loves to teach others about some spiritual values. It mustn't be moralising or rendering the perspective of my own life values.

No wonder I learned English so well as self-taught. Jupiter is responsible for foreign languages and affairs. I can quickly learn other languages. This planet is very fond of travel, language, and knowledge of different cultures. It can indicate marriage to another nationality person, life and success abroad.

Neptune is responsible for philosophy, psychology, all those themes of consciousness, subconscious. As well as creating illusions. It is given to me through Neptune energies to inspire others and motivate. The negative aspect of the illusion could be an addiction. Also, there should be ways to help people take care of them. Neptune is all about caring for others. Being very empathetic and kind-hearted. Neptune is a very female energies planet. It shows that I can sacrifice for the sake of a noble cause. But there is also my Lilit. So I have to be careful that my sacrifice mustn't be inadequate. I can easily fall into a victim's mentality. There is a threat of drowning or becoming an alcoholic. It is important not to forget about myself, my values, self-love and self-care. Neptune is very fond of water. It would be perfect for me to live near the water or spend a lot of time near where is water. If or when I feel bad, the best thing to do is to have a shower or bath. I have a sensitive sensory reception and good intuition. I intuitively can sense the future, future events. So, I am very good at Tarot cards, as it helps with intuitive reading and feeling.

Sun, Moon, and Retrogradus Saturn share their energies with Neptune, indicating that I do like to be a centre of attention - but not too much. Retrograde Saturn connected to Moon shows that I was/ can be restricted in family and marriage. No freedom was given to me.

As well as, Saturn is responsible for planning, structure, and timing. It is a planet of seriousness, order, and practicality. Retrogrades Saturn can indicate that I am always late and get frustrated. |As it is in Venus orbit, it shows that my feminity can be hidden, and I can struggle to love myself. In marriage, I can be very restricted physically and mentally.

My second centre consists of Venus, Mars, Retrograde Uranus, and Retrograde Pluto. All the planets spin in a circle, so I can sometimes feel like I am running in a process, just like a squirrel spins in a circle and has a hard time stopping. It is crucial to plan my resting times. And be able to stop. The best thing to do is to arrange all activities in the morning.

Venus is a very female planet. It gives a beautiful look, feminine energies, a good sense of beauty, and aesthetics. Here is my Selene too. It gives me success in everything that touches on femininity. It is like an area of my luck or things I can turn to when some things are difficult for me. It can be beauty, aesthetics, creativity, or finances. Venus loves all beauty, and material, earthly pleasures. It is imperative to keep up with the happiness as unhappy Venus begins to turn to the fridge and food for comfort. . It is essential for me to feel needed; otherwise, I can start to become miserable.

Venus, at the moment, is at the point in my life, so now my feminine energy is very empowering. . Interesting, but probably no wonder Venus points to Mars.

And Mars is responsible for technique, combat, military themes, and sharp tools. Since a very feminine Venus lives next door, it is no wonder that I have chosen the profession of a hairdresser with sharp scissors, where beauty and aesthetics. I can efficiently work with females.

Although I can happily be in a male company too, as Mars is a masculine planet. In general, I can be so versatile when communicating. I can easily find common ground with anyone. Some original, unconventional ideas may likely be born for me at work. Mars is a beautiful planet for a job and a career, but it can destroy relationships. Mars women are usually unable to tolerate weak men and tend to do everything themselves. Since I have more planets in the centres, those qualities are not so categorical; they "dilute" between other planets.

Let's move on to Mars. Women who have a Mars in a centre can really be a pain to a man. They never will be happy with what their man is doing. And |I am one of them.

Mars is lightning, energy, warrior. This planet helps start activities, but it can also get angry and ignite like a match. So, a woman with strong Mars powers can become like a general or dog trainer at home. Although Mars provides a great burst of energy to create and start something new in my case, I have an R Saturn that would put lots of straining for me to be brave and do it.

It is crucial to learn not to take all the responsibilities on my own shoulders. And if a man does something wrong in my eyes, I have to stop myself from pointing to him that he did wrong because his answer will quickly be -,, darling, do everything yourself if nothing is right for you! "

Retrograde Uranus is a fascinating planet, extraordinary and non-standard. That is where my originality comes from and makes me unique. Uranus attracts situations that can radically change thinking. R Uranus can cause chaos, unexpected problems, and ruined plans. I can also react to conditions and situations very stormy. R Uranus energies also make me very sensitive. It can throw at me situations where I would have no choice. And sometimes, I can overreact. Just intuitively, listening to my gut get me out of them. If a person doesn't change their mindset, this planet makes it do- it will have no choice. When turning to consciousness self-awareness, R Uranus is a planet of esoterics.

I can have unexpected ideas coming to me that need to be written then and there before I forget. I have powerful intuition with Uranus, Neptune, and Pluto in the centre. These planets provide a direct connection to the Universe. If I get stuck and don't know the possible solution, all I have to do is ask a question, and I will get answers.

And that is why I have chosen to listen and learn the language of a Universe.

Retrograde Pluto is also a planet that sends me so many lessons. If I start living in low energies, this planet produces a great deal of negativity that is useful for me to direct toward creating something incredible.

I tend to accumulate resentment and not forgive easily. I need to learn to forgive, forget and release. R Pluto can provide stress, the tension from which it is not so easy sometimes to get out. Sometimes I can feel powerless due to an R pluto sending its,, love" my way. Although I do not like scary movies, I love crime dramas.

This planet encourages spiritual transformation. If I am living in negativity, it will quickly send some challenges my way for me to transform and get out of them. So, I must take care of my mind, thoughts, body, and Soul.

R Pluto loves the felling of ground, earth. So, it is beneficial for me to spend lots of time in nature.

R Pluto had its most substantial time when I turned 44. And that was when Covid 19 hit at its most challenging, and we all went into lockdown.

That was when I started to think about where I was going in my life.

I have a very high intellect but not much inside resources. Mars, with its powerful energies, does help me there. But I do have to put in some work, while everything seems to flow so easily for the others.

My Retrogradus Saturn plays a significant role in my inner self-love journey. For as long as I remember, I never have loved myself. And it takes daily reminders to make me feel good about myself.

R Saturn does not help with any fears - it does strengthen them even more. It can be any fear. In my case - I am afraid of deep water, heights, speed, loneliness, critic. I like being in control of everything and anything. And if I am not- it makes me panic, frustrated, anxious. As R Saturn is in Venus orbit, I often feel worried about my finances. It is important to fight those fears and learn to control them. Go and do no matter how afraid I am.

I can have my financial abundance by using my talents and gifts honestly.

Although not in the centre of my formula, Mercury makes its own little centre as it is in its own orbit. This indicates that I love being surrounded by people. I am an excellent communicator, have strong logic and can think quickly. I have thick and beautiful hair.

North node shows my karmic mission to be the guide, a guru, and a teacher. Share wisdom with society, friends, and family. Teach my own children.

Chiron key is sending its support to Mars, giving me the ability and power to be a pioneer, spreading knowledge about Soul Formula in other countries. At the moment, it is only in Russia, Lithuania, and that part of the world. So, it is my life mission to share this knowledge. To help and encourage others to know their life mission.

So, this is just an abridged version of how I can analyse someone's characteristics by looking at its Soul Formula. I can explain what best professions can be chosen to thrive in. Where does it need to improve in life to be and feel happier. Where and when to be careful. I can explain why your child has a different sense of humour, that for others, it does not seem to be funny.

By looking and analysing the position of planets, I can see if there is any danger or threat and where it can come from.

There is something else to be mentioned as it is much important.

A coin has two sides. There is black, there is white. Dark and light. Cold and hot. So do planets have negative and positive energies. You might discover that you already have lived through some. Learned some lessons. Maybe you are still struggling with others.

I have a twin brother who has identical Soul Formula as mine. But we were living in different energies of the planets. For example - once, he was an alcoholic. Negative point of Neptune. He loved sports. I hate it.

He does not believe in esoteric stuff, so he keeps having challenges. But he loves working in the fields. He used to work in the woods. Can you see where I am going with this?

But... it is not enough just to know about yourself. There is some work to be done too.

To live a harmonious, happy and fulfilled life, one needs to use all the tools one can find and get.

I have a coach that helps me when I start hitting a wall. Lucy helps me when I am down in the dumps. She supports me with the knowledge and tools she has gathered together in her life journey.

She is all excited and happy about my achievements.

Humanity is a race that can not happily be lonely. Everyone needs support in hard times and charing when at its best.

It is not just a Soul Formula I have been studying too. I was searching for a way to harmonise and strengthen those weak planets in my chart. How I could make it all work in my favour.

And in all that I have discovered...

 "All roads lead to Rome"!

Most of the time, I live in a dream world. That is what I was thinking for a long, long time. But...I have realised that being into all esoteric stuff, including astrology, Vedic astrology, numerology, and Tarology, made me discover - that once born to be a Lion, it will not be a Pisces. For example, I have always thought that having a birthday in mid-March would make me be Pisces. I counted myself being a dreamer. But yet, I have felt like it is not entirely true.

When I was looking into Vedic astrology, I was Cancer due to my Rising star sign. It is all about a family and children. Although, I didn't feel that this describes me entirely to the point either. My Sun is in Pisces, and my Moon is in Aquarius. All three of them are water elements. None of them is in Fire or Air elements. See where I am going with this?

My Soul Formula's strongest planets Jupiter and Neptune, are all about spirituality, compassion, addiction, dreaming and love.

So, for me to be able not just to tell my clients why they are the way they are but to help them overcome those obstacles. I needed to have tools and methods to do that.

Now I have gathered everything that I need to be able to help those lost Souls to live with purpose and harmony. I have been there. I did it. I have lived a life where I didn't know where I was going. My job would satisfy me for a while, but I would get bored of it. Now I know why I have felt this way. When I wanted to have a career, but same time a family, children - nobody would understand me. If you're going to have a baby, you should be staying at home, mum. When you can't understand why life throws so many challenges, do you feel that way? Does it sound like you?

There is an explanation and reason for it. Maybe you're working in a job where you don't feel happy? Perhaps this particular job is not written in stars for you at all.

Or maybe you are working in a team and would like to know how to approach a particular person? Or perhaps you own a business and wonder what promotion or working field your employee would be best at?

How would it feel if you could understand why your teenage child makes funny faces that, for you, do not seem to be funny.

When the teacher in a school says - your child is daydreaming most of the time in their class, you would know why is that. It is because Neptune is ruling and sending its energies. Would it help if you would know that he has strong Uranus in the centre while Sun is in Uranus orbit, which makes him have a peculiar sense of humour?

What about that beautiful girl you have and would like her to be like a princess, but all she wants to do is run wild with boys. It indeed indicates her Mars ruling over other planets.

Maybe you would like to discover why your partner is so sensitive all the time? Perhaps, they have Moon in the centre? And for them, it is not a career the most important thing in their life but their children and family.

When a Lilit is blocking Sun energies, you most likely lose your father early in childhood or don't have an excellent relationship with your father. Sun represents your father and your relationship with him.

As well, it can represent the energies of enemies around you. Jealousy, gossip, fake friendships.

This is just the tip of the iceberg, as I love saying. The science of esoteric is so fascinating, and it leads one to learn about its Soul journey in this lifetime. It can help with so much more.

And when you know what and how to do those lessons, life becomes a happy and abundant place to live.

Do you believe in a Soul Journey? Are you an awakening spiritual woman?

If you are struggling to find your happy ending, your happy place to work and live, let's see if I can help you with it.

ABOUT THE AUTHOR

TERESA MURRAY

Teresa is a Soul Destiny Coach helping spiritually awakening women to uncover and live their true purpose with more intention, meaning and success.

While searching for her own Soul calling and meaningful life to live, Teresa went and did so many courses. She has done countless hours of research. She has got herself a few coaching courses. But it was not what she really enjoyed doing, as she felt there was much more.

After discovering Soul Formula in Astro psychology, she finally knew that this was what her own Soul Journey was searching for. When she works with clients and tells them all about it, her Soul sings out of joy. Do something that does not feel like a job, a challenge to live and brings so much fun and happiness. And that is what life is about it.

While leveraging all the tools Teresa has up in her sleeves, she helps those women harmonise the energies of their planets. Live in harmony with Universe while learning lessons of life.

Let's get all these little different paths leading Rome to one clear, beautiful, joyful road to that final destination.

If you're very fascinated with Soul Formula and want to know about yours, come and work with her, Soul Sister.

Teresa is offering 20% off with code SOUL20 for readers of this book on the first 90 min quick Soul Formula analyses call when booking through her website:

www.soul_destiny_coach.com

You can find out more about Teresa in her first collaboration book

www.lulu.com/en/gb/shop/teresa-murray/there-she-glows/paperback/product-7zn4e2.html

Get in touch at:

Email: yoursouldestinycaoch@gmail.com

 facebook.com/teresa.murray.5

 instagram.com/soul_destiny_coach

THE KEY TO HEALING

VICTORIA IRELAND

DEDICATION

This is dedicated with Thanks and Love to…

My Mum who has been my rock throughout. Thank you for all your love and support and for being The Best Mum and Nan in the World. You have been there for us throughout the toughest of journeys. You have lifted us through the lows and cheered us along the highs.

We love you more than the world, Victoria, Zack and Darcey xxx

To my Children, believe in yourself always and most importantly Love yourselves! Never be any one but yourself, and remember you are the writer of your own life story! Never let anyone else hold the pen! I wish you a life full of Love and the tools to get through all the challenges in life and the resilience to triumph through adversity. Your super power is your uniqueness, your authentic selves. You are love and you continue to teach me the wonder of Life and Love every day. xxx

You were Born to Shine!

X

~

You are unique!
Your finger prints will not be repeated!
The chances of you being you and being alive is one in 400 Trillion!

This is for people who have gone through any kind of trauma in their life or who have experienced any abuse. I want to share my story with you to help you with your healing process. I want to be an example to you so that you can have peace and joy in your life again and can thrive! You have survived the worst and now it is time for you to thrive! You define your own life and shape your own future. It may not feel like that at the moment. You may feel like I did at the beginning of my journey, completely and utterly power-less. However, I just didn't realise the power I had within me and the choices I could make. I read so many self-help books, did courses and had years of counselling. All of this did help me and contributed to this healing journey. I took all the best bits from what I picked up along the way and put it in to my own healing journey. This is how I got my power back, how I got control back over my life after years of depression and living in fear after leaving an abusive relationship. This is how I re-trained my brain, became aware of causes, patterns of behaviour and methods to change. This is how I healed, learned to forgive and how I finally managed to pursue my dream of becoming a writer and being able to reach out to others and help them on their journey to their best life. This is how I discovered the central and most important thing in absolutely everything and the key to a happy full life...Self Love! I hope this helps you discover things about yourself you never knew and gives you methods and ways to heal and recover from the traumas you have experienced. This is how you take your power back my friend. I will start at the beginning...

When I was a little girl I was quite the Tom Boy, I loved nothing better than being outside playing amongst nature and to my Mother's horror getting my pretty girly clothes as muddy and grubby as possible. As soon as I got in from School I would go outside to play with the children in the village and loved living in the countryside, having the freedom that it offered. We would walk our two Corgi's through the lush long grass in the field next to our home. When the grass grew long our Corgis would bob up and down like leaping hairy caterpillars trying to get a view of the world above. One year I think the farmer had thought he had been visited by an alien spaceship as without realising we had created several perfect crop circles whilst playing. I always wanted to be out playing using my imagination to create characters and magical imaginary worlds. I also had a great love of animals. We always had a dog and a Cat or two growing up, hamsters, budgies, goldfish, rabbits, guinea pigs and several rescued wild animals too! They meant the world to me and were part of the family. One day I discovered my Cat with a field mouse dangling lifeless from either side of her mouth. I thought it must be dead, but I managed to persuade her to drop it for some rather tasty Tuna and managed to grab an empty Tupperware tub to contain it. I would keep them and endeavour to nurse them back to health and release them back in to the field across the road. Some made it, some didn't. Those that didn't would have a full burial and a service of songs and prayers conducted by myself. With all the family pets we had owned over the years our garden turned in to somewhat of a Church Yard for pets. My Dad would be instructed to dig the graves and mum would buy pretty plants to be planted above. I was a very emotional child that had empathy for others suffering.

The reason I am giving snap shots in to my life is because it is very important for you also to revisit your childhood; the good and the bad parts. To live means we will experience great things but we will also experience great pain. We can't live without experiencing both. There is no way we can avoid pain throughout our life that is why it is so important to learn how to cope with it. It is completely ok to keep learning. We can't be perfect. There is no end goal. As they say, life is a journey not a destination. All we can hope for is that we continue to grow and to learn and try our best! We haven't failed if things still affect us. Our reactions to our experiences are completely normal and valid.

According to research trauma between the ages of 0-7years old impacts how we view ourselves and the world throughout our adult life. Without us investigating this we cannot become aware of our actions and reactions. It is so helpful to question these and realise how and why our lives may have been shaped as they have been up until now. We then have the power to write a new narrative when we have become awakened to our previous one.

At the age of 39 I have finally discovered why I have had a lack of love for myself all my life. I have realised why I ended up in abusive relationships. I realise my childhood between 0-7 had a big impact and also my childhood beyond that point. I am in no way blaming or pointing the finger at my parents for this as they are people in their own right with their own traumas and their own pasts which impacted on their lives. I love my parents deeply and am grateful to all they have done for me in my life. They have been amazing and wonderful loving, hard-working, devoted and nurturing parents. I do not want to take away from this. When I was growing up I was sexually abused at the age of 4 by my friends' older brother. I was round at their house playing and we were not being supervised by her parents. We were left alone for long periods of time when I went round to play. This is something my own parents were not aware was happening when I went round to play. I was very distraught about what happened and felt completely helpless to stop it. I was told to lie down in a cupboard and be still. I did everything they asked and froze. I didn't shout for help or say no. I knew it was wrong and afterwards I felt very dirty. When I got home I told my parents. They reassured me that I'd done nothing wrong and that this shouldn't have happened to me. They told me they would go round to my friends' house and discuss it with her parents and the older brother. At first I was afraid and didn't want them to, but I felt a strong sense of protection from my parents and that this was the right thing to do. This was my first experience of trauma and justice. The result was a feeling of injustice. The boy being told off didn't take away what had happened to me. I had no apology. I lost my best friend and couldn't go round to play with her anymore and was called a liar by others about what had happened. I then had to live with a secret. I couldn't tell people why I was quieter than usual. I felt enormous shame. I had to walk past the house where it happened every day for the next 20 years picturing what happened. To adults it may have seemed like nothing, children being children and just experimenting, but for me, it took my childhood away. I remember the boy being renowned for being good at football and getting lots of praise and recognition. One time at the end of my piano lesson my teacher showed me a newspaper with his photo on it and said, "he lives near you doesn't he" I just nodded. "He has won a trophy, he is an excellent foot-baller isn't he?", said my Piano teacher. I claimed not to know him. I was 10 years old at this point and still struggling to process my pain. I wonder if I had been offered coun-selling now if it would have helped. I was petrified as a child to speak to anyone outside of my mum and dad so I am not sure how much I would have engaged with it. I am just sad it took so many years of my life still living with that feeling of being powerless, feeling guilty, dirty, and ashamed. I believe now this was the start of my lack of self-love.

Growing up in many ways my parents were a great team, although they had quite a volatile relationship, which made me feel insecure and unsafe. Weekends could be absolutely wonderful or absolute hell. They had a lot of pressure on them in various ways, what with providing for three children, keeping a home, cars and accommodating my Nan in to our lives. My Nan was a wonderful inspiration to me and was an incredible mother and Nan. She was like a second mother to me and I feel so blessed she came to live with us. It wasn't easy for her living with a young family. I was 4 when my Nan came to live with us and she was 76. I think it is so important to look at your parents and care givers as people and investigate their upbringings as you can discover a long line of patterns and traumas that impacted the way they lived and their coping mechanisms. My Dad wasn't a very tactile person. He showed love by the things he did for us. He always responded to a hug if I went up to him to give him one but it didn't come naturally to him. This I feel made me feel a sense of rejection at times and also the feeling of abandonment. I became an excellent negotiator and learned how to trigger emotions in people to persuade them not to leave, not to give up and to see how loved they were. I never saw my parents be affectionate to one another and I often had the role of buying birthday cards and gifts for my Mum from my Dad as he would forget. My Mum was a very loving and affectionate person and was very thoughtful in every way and such occasions meant a great deal to her. I discovered that Dads family never made much of birthdays or anniversaries and that he never received much affection himself as a child. It was only as an adult I came to understand how this impacted Dad and it eased the sense of feeling unloved at times or rejected. It wasn't personal towards me, he just didn't know how to show love in this way. I knew deep down my Dad loved me as he would fix up my bike, take me to violin lessons, pick me up from Hockey, take me on long walks with the dogs across the countryside, help me with my maths homework, be Dad's Taxi and would bring me a cup of tea and a biscuit up each morning! He worked long hours to provide for us and we always had old cars that he would have to spend many hours repairing to save money. It was quite a traditional relationship as mum always did all the washing, the ironing, the cooking and childcare. Dad's dinner was always on the table when he got in from work. Mum would play with me for hours and we never went without. We were read to at bedtimes and I have great memories of caravan holidays in Wales. I often wonder if the pressures that society puts on families had been less perhaps they wouldn't have rowed so much and if they had, had the time to do some self -love healing work they wouldn't have passed on their un-dealt with traumas on to their children and it wouldn't have affected their relationship with one another as much as it did. This is why I feel it is so important to do this healing work, to not only heal ourselves and our relationships, but to heal our children, and our childrens' children.

My upbringing was also one of compassion and empathy for others. My mum was a humanitarian and always helping those less fortunate and charitable causes. We were brought up to have a strong social conscience. We were taught to share and not be selfish and were taught to get involved with our local community. My Mum was an especially selfless individual and would put everyone else's needs before her own, but often to her detriment. Although this is a wonderful attribute it also taught me that looking after yourself may be deemed as selfish or indulgent. I often felt frustrated and confused that my mum didn't care for herself in the way she cared for others. She would in many ways neglect herself and I felt it was then my responsibility. My Mum would take everyone to the Doctors but herself! Mum struggled with her deep emotions and this impacted her weight. Mum was always overweight and growing up I could sense how her low self-worth and the judgements and criticism from others upset her tremendously. From a young age I wanted to defend my mother and protect her from negative comments and feared she would die due to her poor health. I watched her relationship with food and fad diets and how she used food to comfort herself when she was upset in any way. I saw her struggle in discomfort at basic tasks and struggle for breath if we walked far. Mum couldn't take us swimming but she always made sure we didn't miss out and that Dad would take us. Mum felt self-conscious about doing most things so would shy away from them. I witnessed how much society labels people and how mum would be seen as lazy, ugly, greedy, unworthy, uneducated and unequal and she was none of those things. It really made me angry at the world that my beautiful, kind, generous, hard-working, highly educated and talented mum could not be seen for what she was and is!

This I believe contributed also to my own self-sabotage. It has taken me until I am 39 to realise it is ok to put yourself first and it is not selfish to do so. I have learnt that we shouldn't seek external validation and it doesn't matter what others think of us. Not saying it still doesn't hurt if other people make negative and harsh comments about us, but that we don't have to allow it the power to affect us as we are so assured of ourselves and love ourselves for who we are that we have roots as strong as a great oak tree that cannot be broken or pulled down. It also taught me the importance of what is on the inside and to be less judgemental of others. I think it is so important to educate ourselves in this way. Don't be what Society says you should be! Be you as much as you can be! There is only one you after all. Don't waste your life trying to live someone else's life.

Our experience of School and friendships also shapes our life. As the hierarchy of needs demonstrates, we need to feel part of a tribe or community, we need to feel valued, accepted and we need friends to prosper in life. I was very much a people pleaser growing up and constantly sought external validation. I put teachers on pedal stools and desperately wanted their approval and praise. I wanted to feel I was good at something. I wanted to be liked. Teachers have the power to make or break us and they have the power to ignite our interest in a subject or completely flatten it. I have great admiration and respect for teachers and always will do, however, I do think we need to take away some of the power they have over our lives. I feel it is important to recognise that teachers are people too and they also make mistakes and are imperfect. I truly believe being imperfectly perfect human beings is what we should recognise ourselves as. Striving to be better and always learning and growing is wonderful and is what I live my life by. However, striving for perfection is not my aim anymore. Striving to be better than I was yesterday yes and not comparing myself to others, comparing myself to myself is my method now. When I went to Primary School I felt invisible to my teacher who was also the Head teacher of the school. It was a very small primary school I went to in a tiny village. This teacher was always praising others around me and I felt she even disliked me and I never understood why. I felt I needed that praise and recognition as I was not strong within myself. I began to feel bad about myself. I felt useless, rubbish, unlikeable, unimportant and invisible. This teacher then retired and a new teacher/head teacher began. My life at school changed overnight. All of a sudden I was great at this and great at that and I was being commended for my work. I felt important again and I felt a strong sense of wanting to help others in the class who were struggling. This teacher was amazing and he really developed my love of learning again. The sadness is that when you are a child people really have the power to make or break you. If only we had the power then to be so self-assured and full of self-love that we believed in ourselves and our own strengths and weaknesses and that we owned them ourselves. It has taken me 39 years to do this. I just don't want my children going through the same. We are all good enough! We are all worthy! We all have strengths! And don't worry if you don't know what yours are yet. I hope reading this will make you look closely at yourself and begin to recognise your own strengths for yourself.

It is wonderful to be a person who encourages others and wants to help others rise. I feel that is the kind of person I always strive to be. It is important to understand your personality traits and characteristics. It helps us to understand what we want back from the world. However, when we don't receive what we give out it can break us. We need to realise not everyone can be this type of person. Not everyone has dealt with their own issues and perceptions. Some teachers may have felt by being harsh brings out the fighting spirit in an individual, because that's what made them strong? We all have our previous experiences that impact our belief systems. What I now say to my children is that they must have respect for teachers and other adults but that adults don't always know what is best. That they are to believe in themselves and their own abilities and strengths and that even teachers and adults make mistakes. I realise as a parent I had children to give them a life. I didn't create them to be robots and not to think independently. I want them to make up their own minds about the world, religion, people, life etc... All I can do is give them the opportunity to experience as many things and situations as possible and show them what I have decided but that there are more options out there. My views and perspectives don't have to be the same as theirs. I want them to not go through the destruction I have been through. I know I can't protect my children from pain as it comes with the gift of being alive. However, I can help them learn methods to deal with it and to be so full of self-love that others won't be able to bring them down or destroy their spirit. This is what I want for you. Believe me when I say this, it is never too late! I am 39 and still learning and my mum is 75 and still learning. We are never the finished article. We are always a work of progress. The reason I say 'of' progress and not 'in' progress is because the word 'in' suggests something wrong with us as we are. The word 'of' suggests we are worthy as we are but we are forever evolving and growing.

At School I think I struggled with friendships. I felt the bitch-iness that went on between girls and the fall outs of one minute being best friends and the next being the worst thing on the planet. I often found myself wanting to be liked, to make people laugh, to be good looking and popular...I wasn't. At secondary School I guess I was labelled and grouped as quite geeky. I had acne, a terrible haircut and clothes that didn't make me stand a chance of being with the 'in' crowd. I felt ugly compared to all the popular girls and when I did get a boyfriend he cheated on me with my best friend. Life was complicated at school. The only saving grace was I loved learning and enjoyed School dinners. I also had some incredible teachers who really inspired me and encouraged me. However, there were still a few teachers that impacted me and prompted me to make rash decisions in an attempt to make them notice me and prove them wrong. At Sixth form my art teacher graded me very low and I felt incapable, not good enough, that I shouldn't pursue art and that my grades were a reflection of my low talent. I decided I would apply to study a further education course in art to prove him wrong and I planned it in my mind that I would get a high grade and go back there a year later to prove to him that I was now a' good' artist. I wasted months applying for a course I didn't need or want to do. I had plans to go into business with my mum. Although I was still hell bent on seeking external validation and approval. Why? We have to ask ourselves why we do this and why we let others affect us so deeply. For me it all comes down to a lack of self-love. If I was so sure of myself I wouldn't have needed his approval or recognition. I still do art to this day and often sketch or paint. I now share my art on Facebook and yes it is lovely to have people comment and say how good something is or that they like my work, but for me art is about expression and being totally submerged in the moment of creation. I use my art to relax and loose myself in. When I am doing my art I am not thinking about anything other than creating and that is wonderful.

School, College and University was a time of wanting to be accepted and fit in and again we are judged by our peers for mostly external things. None of this matters but we put so much emphasis on these external things. We also feel that popularity will deem success. We can all think back to the most popular people in School and when we bump in to them years later we realise they are only people at the end of the day. How do we define success? Again that is a very important question for you as an individual! So, whilst on the topic, how do you define success? For some people it may be being a millionaire, having possessions, having good looks, having a flash car? For me I think I am a successful person because I have triumphed over adversity. I have not let my past define me. I have achieved a BA Honours Degree. I have love in my life in the way of family and friends. Therefore I deem myself as successful.

The key points I would like you to get from this section is looking back and becoming aware of your experiences at school, good and bad and how those may have affected you. I want you to realise how others can make or break us when we give them the power to do so. I want no one to be able to make or break your life again and I want you to regain that power. Your life is in your control and only you can create your life and your future.

Life in general is tough. I think by telling someone life isn't going to be tough is doing them a disservice. Being abused in any way is awful, whether it is physical or mental, it is equally damaging. Words and names can stick in your head for a lifetime. We need to address this internal dialogue in our heads and ask who is saying this? Is this inner critic the voice your Ex-partner? A work colleague? A teacher? A parent?. I just want to make you aware of this. Let me ask you this now. Is what they said true? Do you honestly think it is true? Picture yourself as a child being bullied by those people. How would it make you feel if you witnessed that happening to a child? Imagine yourself at that age? What else could you have done to deal with the situation? I will tell you… you couldn't have done anything else. You dealt with it the best you could with the resources you had at the time. What would you have expected a child that age to do? Exactly! They couldn't have done anything else. Be kind to yourself. Hold yourself in your arms and say I am here for you, I will keep you safe, you are amazing, you are beautiful, you're loved.

The reason I wrote this all stems from my own personal experiences of abuse and personal life experiences. Without realising the inner warrior power I had to take back control of my own life up until recently, I wanted to help reach out to help others. I was completely trapped in my past traumas until the tools I gained from counselling and courses on personal development taught me how I could finally be set free from my internal prison. This has impacted the rest of my life so positively I wanted to share it with others. I can now piece the puzzle together which has helped me in my healing and enabled me to gain a life worth living, not just surviving, but thriving! I run a group on Facebook and Instagram called *The Warrior Within* where I work with various victims of abuse and work on rebuilding their self-esteem and self-love. I also like to raise awareness and help educate people and empower them to use their own inner warrior to live their life to the full.

ABOUT THE AUTHOR

VICTORIA IRELAND

Victoria Ireland is a Freelance Writer and Wellbeing Mentor who helps people via Social Media platforms and via face to face personalised sessions; tailored to the individual.

Before embarking on her career in writing and wellness, Victoria worked as a Business Development Manager. After several personal life challenges and set backs with her own health and well-being, Victoria decided to invest in self-development courses, counselling, personal training and did a lot of soul searching, self love and healing work. After seeing the benefits to her own life and finally being able to follow her dreams in writing and helping others. Victoria decided to embark on establishing her Facebook Page The Warrior Within as a place to help and heal others and reveal to them their own inner Warrior.

Victoria enjoys her time in nature in Rural Shropshire with her two children and many pets.

Victoria is available for writing projects, workshops as well as private consultations.

You can reach Victoria at:

Email - v.ireland82@icloud.com

 facebook.com/The-Warrior-Within-103806142317471
 instagram.com/the_warrior_within_official

Printed in Great Britain
by Amazon

82093759R00154